From the Tables

of

Lebanon

Dalal A. Holmin
Maher A. Abbas, M.D.

Book Publishing Company
Summertown, Tennessee

Cover art and interior illustrations: Kim Trainor
Cover design: Bev Lacy, State of the Art
Interior design: Warren Jefferson

Published in the United States by   Book Publishing Company
                                      PO Box 99
                                      Summertown, TN 38483

ISBN 1-57067-040-4

Holmin, Dalal A., 1951-
      From the tables of Lebanon / Dalal A. Holmin, Maher A. Abbas.
            p.   cm.
      Includes index
      ISBN 1-57067-040-4 (alk. paper)
         1. Vegetarian cookery. 2. Cookery, Lebanese. 3. Lebanon--Social
      life and customs.   I. Abbaas, Maher A., 1966-   . II. Title.
      TX837.H629   1997
      641.5'636'095692--dc21

Note: Lebanon is a culturally diverse country. Because of the regional differences in customs and traditions within Lebanon, some of the dishes included in this book can be prepared in several different ways.

The information in this book is true and complete to the best of our knowledge. All recommendations are made without guarantees on our parts as the authors. We disclaim all liability in connection with the use of this information.

Calculations for the nutritional analyses in this book are based on the average number of servings listed with the recipes and the average amount of an ingredient if a range is called for. Calculations are rounded up to the nearest gram. If two options for an ingredient are listed, the first one is used. Not included are fat used for frying, unless the amount is specified in the recipe, optional ingredients, or servings suggestions.

We would like to dedicate this book to the following people:

From Dalal: to my wonderful husband Leon and my four sons Lieutenant Mohammad Ali, Mazen, Landon, and Zane.

From Maher: to my sweet grandmother Em-Shafiq, to my perfectionist mother Rafica, to my kind father Aref, to my wonderful and affectionate sisters Dalal, Siham, Samar, and to my four gifted brothers Nabil, Chaouki, Mohammad, and Hussam.

May we all be united in Mom's kitchen again.

We are indebted to the following people for their help in testing the recipes and for their support: The Lebanese American Association of California, Dr. & Mrs. Ralph and Marilyn Spiegl, Mrs. Dora Christopherson, Dr. & Mrs. Gregory and Cristina Lackides, Dr. Nadim Maalouf, and Dr. Michel Nabti.

Contents

Preface

In March of 1995, I attended a health and nutrition convention in Anaheim, California, to sign copies of my book *Olive Oil Cookery: The Mediterranean Diet*. After a long day of work and fun, I joined Bob Holzapfel and Warren Jefferson from The Book Publishing Company for a vegetarian meal at a local Mexican restaurant. The food was delicious and we had a great time. During our conversation, Bob had commented on the wealth and diversity of vegetarian cuisine around the world. He also asked me if I would be interested in writing a book about the vegetarian cuisine of Lebanon, my native country. His request was an initial surprise to me. As a medical doctor, I had written my cookbook to show the health benefits of an olive oil-based diet and how it protects against common diseases such as heart disease and cancer. Even though it is a cookbook, I had considered it as part of my medical work. However, I thought about Bob's proposal for a few minutes, smiled, and agreed to do it!

The vegetarian diet of Lebanon is a very healthful one. Since it is mostly an olive oil-based diet, I felt that it would be congruous with my initial medical work. But, most importantly, I saw in it the opportunity to share with fellow Americans and Lebanese the wealth of a very special cuisine. Having traveled extensively around the world, I had no doubt in my mind that the cuisine of Lebanon is one of the most diverse. The basis of this delicious food goes beyond the borders of that small country; it is rooted in three major continents and spans over thirty thousand years of history.

After accepting Bob's challenge, my goal was to write a book that would be useful to any person interested in learning about this fascinating and delicious cuisine. That is why I asked a superb cook to join hands with me to make this project feasible—my oldest sister, Dalal. Prior to immigrating to the United States, Dalal had undergone rigorous training as a cook—in the kitchen of our home, instructed by my mother, Rafica, and my maternal grandmother, Em-Shafiq. It may not seem to you that such credentials are of great importance, but if you were Lebanese or Mediterranean, you would appreciate the excellence of such training. My grandmother, Em-Shafiq, always took pride in cooking some of the most difficult and delicious dishes. She is currently in her mideighties and has not lost her wit and energy in the kitchen. My mother has always been obsessed with the perfection and authenticity of Lebanese cuisine. After immigrating to the United States, Dalal pursued a formal degree in cooking in Minnesota. Since then, she has held several jobs as a cook.

My collaboration with Dalal goes back thirty years. At the time, I was an infant and she was my teenage sister. More than anyone else, she spent a considerable amount of time feeding me, playing with me, and caring for me. She has been a nurturing force in my life ever since. Her collaboration with me on this project was one more example of our loving relationship as brother and sister. It was a delight working with her, and, quite frankly, I could not have done it without her. The journey we undertook together was a remarkable one: hundred of hours working in the kitchen, endless hours behind the computer, many long distance conversations with family and friends in the United States and abroad, two trips to Minnesota and California, and two unforgettable trips to Lebanon. Together we had a memorable and educational experience.

We are very happy with the final product of our efforts. So are our grandmother and mother! We have done our share of the work; now it is your turn. Put on your apron and enter your kitchen to take your own personal culinary journey. We hope that you will enjoy our dishes from Lebanon.

God bless your food table, and may you prosper in peace and good health.

SAHTEN!

صحتين!

Maher Aref Abbas, M.D.
Cave Creek, Arizona

Lebanon:
The Heart of Biblical Land

*The righteous shall flourish
like the palm-tree: he shall
grow like a cedar in Lebanon.*

Psalms [92:12]

Although this is a book about the vegetarian cuisine of Lebanon, it is important to say a few words about this special country. Almost every American has read, heard, or seen something related to Lebanon, whether in the Bible, in a travel guide, in a history book, or, more recently, in the news. To enhance your enjoyment of the recipes in this cookbook, let us give you a brief introduction to what is known as the heart of the biblical land.

Located on the eastern rim of the Mediterranean basin, Lebanon is the link between three major continents: Europe, Asia, and Africa. It is known as the vital heart of the Middle East.

Contrary to what some Americans believe, Lebanon is not a country of desert land. The Arabic word "lebnan" (Lebanon) means white in the ancient language of Aramaic. It refers to the mountainous terrain covered with white snow every year until late springtime. Lebanon offers diverse landscapes from Mediterranean beaches to pine forests. Roughly the size of Connecticut, it has a very narrow coastal plain and, in most instances, the edge of the mountains extend to the sea. Two large chains of mountains, named Mount Lebanon and Anti-Lebanon, run parallel to each other from north to south. Some of their highest peaks extend beyond three thousand meters, roughly about ten thousand feet. Snow covers the mountains of Lebanon until May, offering great skiing opportunities! Absolutely unforgettable are the famous cedars of Lebanon, which grow at an altitude of eight to nine thousand feet. The cedars are closely connected with Lebanon's long history, symbolizing eternity. In between the chains of mountains lies a very fertile valley, called the Bekaa. It is said that the crops of the Bekaa valley fed the entire Roman empire in ancient times.

Despite over three hundred days of sunshine a year, Lebanon has four distinct seasons. Except for the pine and cedar trees, one can enjoy the changing foliage of many trees in the fall and the smell of orange blossoms which bathes the coast in the spring. In the winter, the coastal region sees heavy rains while the mountains are covered with snow. Summer days tend to be hot in the coastal cities but cool in the villages that cover the hills surrounding most cities and the mountains.

The estimated population of Lebanon is 3,600,000. It is believed that there are over 12,000,000 Lebanese immigrants or descendants from Lebanese origin outside Lebanon, mainly in western Europe, North and South America, Canada, Australia, the Arab countries, and some African countries. The official languages in Lebanon are Arabic and French. Most educated Lebanese are multilingual and speak English as well.

Lebanon is the melting-pot of many civilizations. The concentration of archaeological and historical sites in this small country is the result of its physical invasion by several other countries.

The first known inhabitants of Lebanon were the Semitic Canaanites. The Phoenicians, who are considered by many to be the ancestors of the Lebanese people, followed the Canaanites and were excellent shipbuilders, navigators, and superb traders. Byblos, a small seaport town north of Beirut, is the oldest known city and seaport in the world. The journeys of the Phoenicians took them to other Mediterranean countries, the coasts of Africa, and possibly the eastern shores of South America. After many centuries of prosperity, the Phoenicians were invaded by the Greeks, who gave a new architectural flavor to the coastal cities of Lebanon. The Romans followed the Greeks and were the initial settlers of the mountains.

Christianity shaped the culture of Lebanon under Byzantine rule. Around the seventh century, the spread of Islam brought the Arabs to Lebanon. They dominated Lebanese culture until the arrival of the Crusaders from Europe toward the end of the eleventh century. Their reign over Lebanon did not last long, and in the thirteenth century, the Mongols and the Mamluks came from Egypt and Central Asia and replaced the Crusaders. Toward the beginning of the sixteenth century, the Ottoman empire extended its rule over Lebanon. However, with the slow decline of Ottoman rule at the end of the nineteenth century, France filled in the gap and became the dominant ruler of Lebanon. French domination was short and on November 22, 1943, Lebanon was granted its independence.

Since this time, Lebanon has been trying to acquire its own identity. Unfortunately, little progress has been made due to regional conflicts affecting its politics, the four Arab-Israeli wars, and the more recent civil war (1975-1992). However, since the end of the war in 1992, Lebanon has undergone a period of rapid growth, rebuilding, and modernization. Currently, Beirut is the largest construction site in the world. Once again it is acquiring an image of prosperity and peace. Hopefully, an everlasting peace will bless all the people of the Middle East and bring them together to celebrate their ethnic and religious differences in harmony.

The Lebanese Cuisine and Its Healthful Ingredients

"I like to see my darling Tyro of Lebanon, quenching her thirst from the spring. I would embrace her and say: 'I am a farmer from Lebanon; I know the order of the four seasons and am ready to plough your lands and gather your crops' . . ."

Dionysiaque
Nonos of Panapolis (Greek Poet)

Lebanese cuisine is predominately based on vegetarian dishes, although lamb, fish, and chicken are also used. By far, the majority of dishes are prepared with fresh ingredients bought on a daily basis. Food markets are in great abundance in the coastal cities, and in the small mountainous towns many people grow their own vegetables, grains, orchards of olive trees, citrus, and fruits. Traveling through the countryside of Lebanon in the spring or early summer is a heavenly experience: the smell and sight of blossoming trees, citrus in the south, almond trees in the north, cherry trees in the mountains, and the refreshing Bekaa valley breeze mixed with the scent of soil and white potatoes. The sight of old fishermen rowing their fishing boats on the Mediterranean and the shepherds with their herds of sheep on the hills in the early morning hour make the journey an unforgettable one!

Within the cities, vegetables and fruits are sold in little produce markets called "souk al-khodra" or from vegetable carts pushed around the cities by vendors singing the prices and warning people to hurry before everything is sold out. Only seasonal produce is available, as the Lebanese are not accustomed to importing chemically grown vegetables from other countries. Traditionally, summer and early fall are the times during which most Lebanese stock up on their winter food supplies. Although this practice was crucial to survival, especially in the mountains where winters can be very harsh, it is no longer a necessity. However, the tradition continues. Most families keep busy pickling vegetables, putting up jam and honey, finding good quality olive oil from their regional area, and searching for spices, herbs, and bulgur. As any visitor would attest, when entering a Lebanese kitchen one will encounter large jugs filled with olive oil, big jars of pickled cucumbers, turnips, olives, cabbage, eggplants, and jars of jam and honey. Also, there will be many cotton bags filled with bulgur, spices, and dried fruits, especially walnuts, pine nuts, figs, and peaches.

The ingredients used in Lebanese cuisine are too numerous to describe in this book. Rather, we have included some basic items which are most commonly used and which have received recent medical attention. As we mentioned before, the cuisine of Lebanon is a very healthful one, and the Lebanese in general enjoy good health, with much lower rates of heart disease and cancer compared to the Western world, including the U.S.

Olive Oil

Olive oil is the essence of Lebanese cuisine. Several large jugs are consumed each year in every Lebanese home. It is used in cooking grains and vegetables, mixed with herbs and raw produce, poured over yogurt dishes, dipped with bread, spread on herbal pies and pizzas, and added to many baked dishes.

Historical uses

Olive trees and olive oil have existed since prehistoric times. Olive trees are remarkable for their longevity; trees as old as five hundred years are common. Known to many of the ancients as the queen of all trees, olives were probably first cultivated in Palestine around the fourth millennium B.C. Ever since the Golden Age of Greece, there has been a demand for olive oil reaching from one end of the Mediterranean to the other. Amphoras, jars used for olive oil storage, are one of the most common objects found in the remains of ancient Greek shipwrecks.

From the earliest times, olive oil has been used for many things other than food. The Egyptians used it for preserving mummies, and throughout the ancient world medicinal uses were common—as therapy in the treatment of cancer and for most common ailments, as well, ranging from diarrhea to constipation, and from burns to baldness. It is known today that olives contain a compound with antitumor properties, called sitosterol-d-glucoside. Olive leaf extracts have antihypertensive, as well as antibacterial, properties. This may explain why ancient physicians found that its use resulted in general improvement in the health of their hypertensive patients, long before blood pressure could be scientifically measured. Olive oil has also been used in religious ceremonies as part of the act of consecration or anointment, as an ingredient of cosmetics, and as fuel for lamps. Olive branches were used by Egyptians for decorative purposes and by Greeks as symbols of victory in the ancient Olympic games. Later they came to symbolize peace as well as victory, a cultural practice carried over to modern times in the emblem of the United Nations.

The most important use of the products of olive trees was, of course, as food. Along with bread and wine, olive oil was treasured by ancients from the entire

Mediterranean region, and that is still true today. Now this oil, which plays a primary part in the cuisine of so many countries, has emerged as the most healthful cooking oil one can possibly use, by far.

Often scientists make discoveries only to find out that our ancestors had done the right thing without the benefits of modern scientific knowledge. Dr. Ancel Keys once wrote:

"I am reminded of Elie Metchnikoff, the successor to Louis Pasteur as director of the Institut Pasteur. He became fascinated with longevity and visited Greece on that account. He concluded that centenarians were ten times more common in Greece than in France. We may discount his theory that the credit should go to yogurt, a foodstuff then unknown in other parts of Europe. In any case, from many surveys on the island of Crete, starting in 1957, I have the impression that centenarians are common among farmers, whose breakfast is often only a wineglass of olive oil."

Grades and varieties

In Lebanon, most of the olive trees are grown in the coastal regions, although some have been planted at altitudes up to fifteen hundred feet. Olive trees usually bloom in the spring, with harvest reaching a peak during the fall. Olives are green as they emerge from buds, turning to purple and ultimately to black. The pulp is about 25 percent oil. The rest is water, acid, and fibrous residue. Green olives contain less oil, but as they mature and become black, both their oil and acid contents increase. In general, oil from green olives is of a better quality than oil from black olives.

Once harvested, olives can be cured for eating or pressed for oil. Olives destined for oil are first crushed and then pressed. If pressed with mechanical pressure but without heat, the oil is referred to as "first cold pressing." Oil derived from a first cold pressing of green olives is referred to as extra-virgin oil. By definition (at least for oils imported to the United States from Spain, France, and Italy), the extra-virgin grade has less than 1 percent acidity. Further pressing (second and third) leads to oil with higher acidity and, for most purposes, lower quality. Such oil is adequate for cooking, but will not taste as good in salads, marinades, and other uncooked dishes. Oil that is more than 4 percent acidic cannot be used for human consumption. Grades of oil lower than extra-virgin (more than one percent acidic) are classified as follows:

1-1.5 percent—fine virgin
1.5-3 percent—regular virgin
3-4 percent—pure (or virgin)

There is another distinction in grading olive oil: whether or not it has been filtered. Filtered oil is clear but may have less taste than unfiltered oil because some of the more flavorful components have been removed. Labeling can be misleading. Since olive oil is not (as of this writing) regulated by the FDA, it's a good idea to know something about the label and the importer. For example, some oils are being sold as extra-virgin that meet the established criteria only by adding chemicals during the refining process in order to reduce acidity. "First cold pressing," if honestly used together with "extra-virgin," should indicate the highest quality oil.

Olive oils are much like wines in several ways: they are known by their distinct colors, where they are grown, and how they are produced. The color of the oil may vary from yellow to deep green and has nothing to do with quality. Also, there are growing regions that are famous for certain varieties. These orchards (estates) are known for their outstanding quality and have vintage years that are better than others. Like grapes, olives are affected by nuances of soil and climate. There are also subtle differences in flavor and aroma, and (of course!) price. When purchasing olive oil, don't assume that the higher the price, the greater your satisfaction. Like wines, you should be more concerned with your own subjective response and that of your guests. And don't assume that you require an 8-ounce bottle costing $20 for foods that are to be sautéed; save the fine oil for foods that are uncooked!

Cooking with olive oil

Before you start cooking with olive oil, we have a few words of advice about our recipes and how to handle olive oil in your kitchen. It's important to choose the right oil. Remember that the color of the oil cannot tell you much. Olives change color from green to black as the season goes by. Deep green oil is mostly from the early harvest, and yellow oil is from the end. Any other color comes from harvests between these two time periods (but there are exceptions). The rest is largely a matter of personal taste.

For oils that are to be used in uncooked food, it's important to taste several varieties, or at least to get some advice. If there is a store near your home that caters to gourmet chefs, ask them to recommend a couple of oils to try. If there is a high quality Greek, Italian, or other Mediterranean restaurant nearby, ask the chef if you may taste different oils.

Begin your tasting by inhaling the aroma deeply. Then simply take a small amount of oil in a spoon, and place it on your tongue. The back of the tongue is most sensitive to the flavors that discriminate one oil from another. Leave the oil in your mouth for about ten seconds. Then, if you wish to taste another oil, spit out the first sample, clear your palate with a piece of bread, and repeat the test. Just like a wine tasting! If you are left with a bad aftertaste—acidic or fatty—you should try another oil. Remember to look for first cold pressing extra-virgin oil if you wish to use it in uncooked dishes; the less expensive fine or regular virgin oil is adequate for cooking.

Another consideration is whether the oil has been filtered or not. Filtered olive oil often looks transparent, while unfiltered is mostly cloudy. Some people believe that filtering the oil eliminates some of the flavor and deprives the oil of its distinctive qualities.

Be cautious about labeling; some labels are misleading. For example, "light" olive oil does not mean fewer calories than oil that is not so marked. Rather, this term refers to the flavor of the oil. Light olive oils are produced because Americans in general are not used to the distinctive odor of olive oil.

At home, it is best to store olive oil in a glass, glazed clay, or stainless steel container. Don't use iron, copper, or plastic containers. Keep olive oil in a cool, dark place, but not in a refrigerator; cold temperatures will turn it cloudy. Refrigerated oil is also likely to become much more viscous. Before using refrigerated oil, allow it to warm to room temperature.

Garlic

Garlic is an essential ingredient in Lebanese cuisine. Without exception, every Lebanese family uses raw or cooked garlic in their meals. It is primarily grown in the fertile Bekaa valley.

When shopping for garlic, select fresh, firm, plump heads with cloves that are still covered with paper-like peels. Soft, shriveled, or spongy cloves are already spoiled. Garlic should be bought on a regular basis (once every two to four weeks) and stored in a cool, dry place. Garlic is best crushed with a garlic press or a mortar and pestle.

One of the disadvantages of garlic is the strong and distinctive odor it leaves on your breath! To minimize this, cook the garlic instead of eating it raw. Rinsing the mouth with fresh lemon juice, chewing on dill, fennel, or anise seed, eating an apple, or chewing a roasted coffee bean may help decrease the effects of garlic on your breath. A cup or two of White Coffee (*Kahwe Bayda*) page 154, will also help reduce this effect. Try it!

Citrus

Lebanon is famous for its citrus produce. As with olive oil and garlic, lemons, oranges, and grapefruits are consumed on a daily basis. Lemons and their juice are used in almost every Lebanese salad, as a basic component of many marinades, or as a sauce poured on a variety of dishes. Lemon wedges are even eaten raw, dipped in sea salt, especially in the spring. Oranges are freshly squeezed for their juice, as our mother has done and continues to do every morning for our family for the last fifty years! They are also used in a variety of baked goods, including cakes, and served as dessert fruits. But most importantly, orange blossoms are used to make an extract called "mazaher," which is used in syrups, desserts, juices, and some breakfast dishes. In addition to this extract, orange blossoms are used during weddings to perfume the rooms and as a natural alternative to bubble bath.

Lemons should always be squeezed at room temperature in order to extract all of their juice.

Beans and Grains

Beans and grains are in great abundance in Lebanon and represent the heart of Lebanese cuisine. It would be difficult to imagine Lebanese food without them. The most common of these include rice, bulgur (partially cooked, cracked wheat), and beans—chick-peas (garbanzos), fava beans, lentils, black-eyed peas, white beans, and green beans. They are sautéed in olive oil, boiled, baked, or added to a variety of stews. Many of the recipes included in this book will help you discover how good beans and grains can taste!

In addition to their good taste, beans and grains are excellent sources of protein, carbohydrates, and many water soluble vitamins, including some B vitamins. They are very low in fat.

Bulgur *burghul*

Bulgur is a grain which enjoys great popularity in many Middle Eastern countries. It is made by boiling, drying, and then crushing whole wheat kernels. In the countryside, the drying process is done by placing partially cooked kernels in baskets in the full sun. Once dried, the kernels are milled into various grades: coarse, used in pilaf, soups, and stews; medium, for fillings and tabouli; and fine, for salads. Sometimes a very fine flour is made for bread baking. The medium grade is the most popular and the type you will be most likely to find in the U.S.

Chick-peas (garbanzo beans)

Chick-peas are used widely in the cuisine of Lebanon and around the Middle East. They are a good source of calcium and have a little more fat than most legumes. Chick-peas are a very firm legume and need to be soaked overnight (or at least eight hours beforehand) if you're going to cook them in a saucepan on top of the stove. If you bring them to a boil in the soaking water and simmer for 1 minute, you can reduce the soaking time to 1 hour. If you use a pressure cooker, you can prepare unsoaked chick-peas in 35 minutes and soaked chick-peas in 25 minutes.

If you wish, you can remove the skins from the chick-peas (or any cooked beans) by cooling them until they can be handled and pressing them with your hands or a rolling pin.

Fava beans broad beans or *fool*:

Fava beans are another popular legume in the Middle East. They are either medium brown or creamy in color. They tend to have tough skins, so you may want to remove these skins using the method previously mentioned for chick-peas.

The Health Benefits of Lebanese Foods

Besides being delicious, many of the foods common to Lebanese cuisine are also important for maintaining good health. Doctors and researchers are learning more about the health-giving properties of unprocessed foods and how they can be used to prevent heart disease, cancer, and even help fight the common cold.

Olive Oil

The principal type of fat found in olive oil is monounsaturated fat. There has been a great deal of interest in monounsaturated fats and their potential role in reducing the risk of heart attacks and strokes. These illnesses kill more Americans every year than all the casualties suffered by the United States in all of its wars combined.

Several studies have been conducted in the U.S. and abroad to investigate the relationship between monounsaturated fats and heart disease. Monounsaturated fats, especially olive oil, have been shown to have a much better record than other fats in protecting against this disease when studies involving large numbers of participants were done. One of the best known of these is the Seven Countries Study. Begun in 1958 and continued over 15 years, this study looked at the causes of heart disease and occurances of death from heart attacks. The countries involved were the U.S., Finland, Japan, Italy, Yugoslavia, the Netherlands, and Greece. The initial sample involved more than 11,000 middle-aged men. Researchers tracked several variables: diet, cigarette smoking, blood pressure, weight, and exercise habits. Finland and the U.S. had the highest death rate from heart disease; Japan, Greece, and Italy had the lowest. When all the information on diet was analyzed, several patterns were apparent. A high intake of saturated fats was common in Finland and the U.S., a low-fat diet was eaten by the Japanese, but a high-fat diet (rich in monounsaturated fats) in Greece and Italy seemed to accompany low rates of heart disease in those countries. Olive oil consumption was the key factor.

Following the Seven Countries Study, some critics questioned the idea that diet was the main reason for those lower rates. Could physical exercise account for the difference? Were the Greeks and Italians more active? Dr. Anna Ferro-Luzzi and her colleagues carried out a study in rural southern Italy to investigate the effect of a change in diet on total cholesterol levels, without changing other factors. Animal fats were partially substituted for olive oil for a period of 42 days, without any other changes in lifestyle. The results were astonishing: in just 42 days, both LDL—the "bad" cholesterol—and total cholesterol levels increased significantly!

Recently, several other studies have compared the effects of a high-monounsaturated fat diet and a high- carbohydrate/low-fat diet on total cholesterol and HDL—"good" cholesterol—levels. They showed that while both diets equally lowered total cholesterol, HDL levels fell in the high-carbohydrate/low-fat diet group but did not change in the monounsaturated group. Drs. Mensink and Katan, who conducted one of the studies, concluded in their report:

"The olive oil diet, which combined a high intake of total fat with a low intake of saturated fat, caused a specific fall in non-HDL cholesterol, while leaving HDL cholesterol and triglyceride values unchanged. In view of the supposed anti-atherogenic effect [ability to prevent heart disease] of HDL, reducing total fat intake per se might not be the best way to prevent CHD [coronary heart disease]."

In addition to Drs. Mensink and Katan, several other doctors and scientists have studied olive oil, and all agree on its ability to protect against heart disease. Drs. Frank W. Sacks and Walter W. Willett from Harvard Medical School reported in 1991:

"An alternative to a low-fat diet for lowering cholesterol levels is the traditional Mediterranean diet, which is just as low in saturated fat and cholesterol. In this diet, olive oil is a major source of energy, fats average 35 to 40 percent of total calories, and rates of coronary disease are as low as in populations with very low-fat diets. The Mediterranean alternative—using monounsaturated fat as a major dietary component—appears to be at least as healthful, maybe even a better way to improve the lipid profile [balance of fats in the bloodstream], and will provide more variety and greater satisfaction to many."

In terms of reducing the risk of developing heart disease, a diet high in monounsaturated fat, such as olive oil, is probably more healthful than a simple low-fat diet, which is the type recommended by the American Heart Association. A low-fat diet is good for weight control, but it decreases HDL cholesterol, which is believed to increase the risk of heart disease.

Recently there has been additional interest in olive oil because it contains vitamin E. Many studies have reported that vitamin E can protect against heart disease and cancer. It prevents the formation of dangerous compounds in the body after exposure to harmful pollutants. Two recent studies conducted in Spain and Italy, in collaboration with Harvard University, showed that in the thousands of women studied, olive oil was the key factor in protecting against breast cancer. In addition to protecting against heart disease and cancer, Vitamin E has been useful in reducing blood pressure, healing wounds, helping prevent cataracts, and reducing leg cramps. As more research is conducted, it will be interesting to see what other health benefits may be associated with olive oil and vitamin E.

The Lebanese people, similar to their Greek neighbors, consume a lot of olive oil and enjoy good health.

Garlic

Since ancient times, it has been known that garlic has medicinal properties. It has been used to reduce fever, alleviate the pain of swelling, strained tendons and ligaments, and treat parasitic, bacterial, and fungal infections.

In more recent times, the medical community has invested a lot of research in understanding how garlic affects the human body. Several research studies have investigated the role of garlic as a toxin neutralizer and immune system booster. Fresh garlic contains many sulfur compounds and another compound called allicin. Both of these compounds have some of the properties of modern antibiotics and can treat certain infections. Allicin has been shown to inhibit the growth of bacteria, in much the same way as penicillin.

Garlic can also play a role in decreasing total blood cholesterol as well as blood pressure. Since blood cholesterol and blood pressure are major factors in the development of heart disease, garlic can offer some protection. It is unclear at this point how garlic works, although some people believe that it dilates blood vessels and decreases the tendency to form blood clots. Ajoene, a compound found in garlic, is believed to thin the blood.

The interest generated by recent medical and scientific studies have resulted in an increased use of garlic throughout the world. Many companies have been producing garlic in a pill form. The advantage of such pills is that they do not cause the bad breath that some people experience after eating fresh garlic. The disadvantage of the pills is that we still do not know if they provide the same health benefits associated with fresh garlic.

Citrus

The health benefits of citrus produce are derived from their high content of vitamin C, a nutrient that has been subject to extensive research. The late Dr. Linus Pauling, a two-time Nobel Prize recipient, was a great believer in vitamin C and spent a significant portion of his research career studying it. Vitamin C can protect against a variety of viral infections, including the common cold. In Lebanon, fresh lemon juice is added to tea to help alleviate the discomforts of upper respiratory ailments and treat mouth sores. Many women mix lemon juice with equal parts of honey and apply it as a rejuvenating facial preparation.

Dandelions

Dandelions are good sources of vitamins B and C, as well as alkaline salts which purify the body. It is thought that dandelions help promote healthy circulation and cleanse the skin.

Parsley

Parsley is an herb with a variety of health related benefits. It can improve thyroid problems, reduce indigestion and gas, and alleviate the symptoms of rheumatic disease and menstrual disorders.

Thyme

Thyme is known to have many health benefits, including reducing blood cholesterol, alleviating the respiratory discomforts of sinusitis, asthma, and colds, and helping with headaches and abdominal cramping and gas.

Sumac

Sumac can provide several health benefits that range from boosting the immune system to reducing the symptoms of anemia, fatigue, and diabetes.

Why a Vegetarian Diet?

The health benefits of a vegetarian diet have been recognized for a long time. As researchers continue to study vegetarians around the world, they are learning more about the protective factors of such a diet against cardiovascular disease and cancer.

It is estimated that several million Americans follow a vegetarian diet. Some do so for health related reasons, while others do for religious, ethical, or philosophical reasons. There are a variety of vegetarian styles. Vegans eat only plant foods; no products from animal sources are consumed. A vegan diet will contain no cholesterol and very little saturated fats. Lacto-vegetarians eat dairy products in addition to plant foods. Lacto-ovo-vegetarians eat plant foods, dairy products, and eggs.

It is well known that adults who eat vegetarian diets have a lower risk for cardiovascular disease, hypertension, cancer, diabetes, and obesity (overweight). Having high blood pressure puts one at greater risk for developing heart disease and stroke. The higher the blood pressure, the greater is the risk of suffering a stroke. Several surveys conducted earlier this century suggested that blood pressure levels may be related to the amount of meat in the diet. Epidemiological studies done in the South Pacific Islands, Australia, Malaysia, India, China, Japan, Europe, and the United States have shown a trend linking diets containing fish and only a little meat to low blood pressure. Many questions arose from the above observation. Can blood pressure be altered within a population by changing meat consumption? How about blood pressure in vegetarian populations? A group of lacto-vegetarian college students in California were asked to add meat to their diet. Just 11 days later, their systolic and diastolic pressures started to increase. In Yugoslavia, a group of elderly persons were asked to decrease their meat, fish, and egg consumption to 5 per cent of their total caloric intake. After two or more months of changing their diet, a significant decrease in blood pressure was noted. In addition to the above studies, blood pressure levels in vegetarians have been reported to be lower than levels in the general population. Clearly then, a vegetarian diet does contribute to a decrease in blood pressure which in turn decreases the risk of cardiovascular disease.

The reduction of blood pressure levels is not the only cardiovascular benefit that a vegetarian diet offers. Since a vegan diet has no cholesterol and a vegetarian diet contains very little cholesterol and saturated fats, vegetarians also have lower serum cholesterol. The Framingham Study reported that the higher the serum cholesterol in a population, the greater the risk of suffering coronary artery disease.

Furthermore, the higher the fat intake in a diet, the easier it is to gain weight even if the total caloric intake is the same. How can this be possible? Imagine two people who both consume 2,000 calories a day, but the first person derives 40% of his calories from fat while 10% of the calories of the second person's diet is fat. Assume that both people have the same weight initially, the same lifestyle, and physical activity level. The first person will gain more weight than the second person. It takes less energy (calories) to store fat in the body than it does to store carbohydrates (sugars). Therefore, if both people had an equal excess of calories to store in the body, the first person will easily store the fat calories, while the second person will have to expend some energy to convert the carbohydrates into fat and then store it.

Generally, vegetarian diets are lower in fat than those of meat eaters. Consequently, as a group, fewer of them are obese (overweight) than the general population. Obesity increases the risk of high blood pressure and puts more work on the heart and kidneys. Furthermore, obese people tend to develop adult onset diabetes which may lead to heart disease. In that respect, vegetarians enjoy better cardiovascular health when compared to non-vegetarians.

Since non-vegetarians have a greater risk of developing cardiovascular disease than vegetarians, would that risk decrease if a vegetarian diet was adopted? Even more importantly, can someone who already has cardiovascular disease reduce their chances for heart attacks and chest pain, and be able to increase their physical activity and quality of life by changing their diet? Obviously these are complex and difficult questions to answer, especially since the onset of cardiovascular disease is a slow process that may take several decades to manifest. However, there is some evidence that it may be possible to reverse coronary artery disease by changing one's dietary habits and adopting a more healthful lifestyle.

Recent work by Dr. Dean Ornish has contributed to our understanding of how coronary artery disease can be reversed with lifestyle changes. In his project "The Lifestyle Heart Trial," Dr. Ornish took a group of patients with heart disease and assigned them to two groups. The members of the first group were prescribed a low-fat vegetarian diet, moderate physical exercise, stress management training, smoking cessation, and group support. The control group did not make any lifestyle changes. Both groups were followed for a period of time. A year later, Dr. Ornish observed that the lifestyle change group did better than the control group. He reported that he was even able to *reverse* coronary artery disease in some patients in the experimental group. Overall, heart disease continued to progress in the control group.

Currently, Dr. Ornish is continuing his research and is educating more patients and health care professionals about his health intervention program. So far, one insurance company is willing to reimburse fees for patients interested in enrolling in Dr. Ornish's plan, and several medical centers around the country are considering starting programs modeled after his work. This is very encouraging. To say how much of the success in reversing heart disease is related to a low-fat vegetarian diet is impossible at this moment. However, it is clear that a vegetarian diet, within the context of other lifestyle modifications, is indeed beneficial for one's cardiovascular health and has the potential for reversing already existing heart disease.

How about cancer? Several epidemiological studies have found that vegetarians have lower rates of certain cancers, such as breast, colon, and prostate cancer. For example, the rate of these cancers among Seventh-Day Adventists is lower than in the general population. Members of this religious group abstain in general from smoking and using alcohol, as well as follow a lacto-ovo-vegetarian diet. But even when cancers linked to smoking and alcohol are accounted for, Seventh-Day Adventists still have lower rates of cancer than the general population.

Although their lower rate of cancer deaths may be attributed to eating little or no meat, it is difficult to say how much of this reduced rate may be due to high intakes of cereal grains, fresh produce such as vegetables and fruits, or the avoidance of caffeine. Can the increase in cancer in non-vegetarians be due to growth hormones fed to animals later slaughtered for meat, or can it be linked to some of the preservatives (i.e. nitrites) used to prolong the shelf life of food products? Could the lower rates of cancer among vegetarians be linked to the antioxidant effects of vitamins, such as vitamin E, or to the minerals present in fresh produce? As medical researchers try to answer the above questions and determine the relative contribution of different factors to the incidence of, or protection against, cancer, one fact remains true: the "vegetarian lifestyle" is healthful and decreases the risk of many lifestyle-related cancers.

In addition to the evidence we have from vegetarian groups such as the Seventh-Day Adventists, several studies done on immigrants to the United States from countries such as Japan, Italy, and Greece, have contributed to our knowledge about diet and cancer. For example, it was found in the past that Japanese immigrants have a higher rate of colon cancer when compared to members of their same generation who remained in Japan. It is clear that the lifestyle changes adopted by the immigrants to the United States contributed to this increase in cancer incidence and mortality. Some of these changes included an adoption of a more Westernized diet (high in fat and animal products), a change in physical activity, and a change in family and social support (which may lead to an increase in emotional stress). Therefore, it is difficult to know how much of the increase in their cancer rate was related to diet and how much was related to other factors. However, it is clear that diet plays a significant role.

Any disease has many causes, and it is often a very challenging task to try to establish a simple relationship between cause and effect. However, we do know that cardiovascular disease and cancer kill over one million Americans a year. As medical researchers try to get a better understanding of the causes of heart disease and cancer, it is helpful to know there are ways to protect ourselves and decrease our risk of suffering from lifestyle-related diseases. The choice of how we live remains ours, and the knowledge of modern nutrition and diet is available to guide us. A vegetarian diet has a lot to offer. And, best of all, the delicious variety found in Lebanese cuisine is ideally suited to this healthful vegetarian diet.

Dalal's Hints for Successful Cooking

- Adding fresh lemon juice to omelets, according to your taste, can enhance their flavor.

- Pine nuts are commonly used in Lebanese cuisine to add flavor to recipes. They can be used raw or sautéed until golden in olive oil.

- When using tomato paste, dissolve it in lukewarm water before adding it to your cooking so it will combine more easily.

- When boiling potatoes, always add them to boiling water instead of cold water to help prevent loss of vitamins.

- If a recipe calls for both minced garlic and salt, add the salt to the garlic as you mince it. It will make the garlic easier to chop.

- When preparing a recipe, taste a bit of it as it progresses. Lebanese people do that often and modify the flavors as they go along.

- Spices lose some of their potency over long periods of time. It is best to buy them in small amounts as needed.

- Olive oil is the main oil used in this book. Occasionally, we use canola oil for frying. Try to substitute these two oils for all others (i.e. butter, margarine, palm oil, coconut oil, etc.) in your diet.

- When preparing dishes with pasta, always add a bit of olive oil to the boiling water. It prevents the pasta from clumping and sticking together.

- Fresh yeast should be stored in airtight bags and kept in the refrigerator. It will last up to a month when stored this way.

- Most dough containing yeast should not rest at warm temperatures for more than 45 minutes and for more than 90 minutes at room temperature. Always keep yeast dough covered with a damp cloth to keep it from drying out.

- When possible, always use fresh ingredients instead of canned or preserved ones.

- It is preferable to mix water and a little bit of fresh lemon juice to tahini prior to using it in any of the recipes. This thins the tahini and makes it easier to cook with.

•When cooking with milk or yogurt, stir constantly to prevent scorching.

•When making tahini sauce, always blend water with tahini first, then add lemon juice to make a nice, white sauce. This method applies to any use of tahini paste.

•When I make Mihshi (stuffed vegetables), I like to use Egyptian rice. This rice is available in Middle Eastern stores.

•Always place chopped, sliced, or diced eggplant in salted, cold water before cooking, so the eggplant does not turn dark. This helps reduce the amount of oil the eggplant will absorb when frying.

•To remove the skin easily from a hot baked or broiled eggplant, place the eggplant in a bowl of cold water.

•To ensure your cooked rice will be fluffy, use well-salted hot water and do not stir the rice once the water evaporates.

From the Tables of Lebanon

"If you bake bread with indifference, you bake a bitter bread that feeds but half man's hunger."

—*Khalil Gibran (1883-1931)*
Lebanese-American writer, philosopher, painter

About The Recipes

The following recipes are not etched in stone. The Lebanese people differ in the way they prepare their food in Lebanon. Use the directions as a guide, but don't be limited by them. Adjust the dish as you cook it to meet your own taste. Cooking a dish is an interactive process, and your personal touch will help produce a delicious one.

Regarding the names of the recipes, we have used the original Arabic name written both in Arabic and Roman script, as well as a description in English of each dish. This will prove valuable for Americans interested in the true pronunciation of the recipe names, as well as for Lebanese immigrants (especially the young ones) who are familiar with the Arabic name only.

From the Tables of Lebanon

Basic Recipes

Arabic Bread (Pita)
Khibibz Arabi
خبز عربي

2¼ teaspoons dry baking yeast
1½ teaspoons sugar
1 cup lukewarm water

3 cups flour
1 teaspoon salt
¼ cup milk

Cornmeal

Dissolve the yeast and sugar in a ¼ cup of the lukewarm water. Let stand for 10 minutes.

Place the flour and salt in a large bowl. Make a depression in the center, and add the remaining water, the milk, and dissolved yeast. Begin mixing the flour with the liquid, making sure all the batter on the sides of the bowl is well mixed into the dough. Dip your hands in water, and knead the dough for 10-15 minutes until it is smooth and elastic. Cover the dough and set in a warm place until it doubles in size, at least 2-4 hours.

Punch the dough down and knead for a couple of minutes. Form into 4 smooth balls. Each ball should be the size of an orange. Cover the dough with a cloth, and set in a warm place. Let it rise for 30 minutes.

Preheat the oven to 500°F. Roll out the balls into circles about ¼ inch thick. Place on cookie sheets sprinkled with cornmeal, and place in the middle of the oven. Bake for about 5 minutes, then place the bread under the broiler for a few seconds until lightly browned.

The breads may be eaten right away or frozen for long-term storage. If you are going to store the bread, let it cool down to room temperature for 30 minutes before packing into a plastic bag. Frozen loaves can be warmed in the oven or microwave.

Makes 4 loaves

Per loaf: calories: 321, protein: 10 gm., carbohydrates: 67 gm., fat: 1 gm.

Bulgur Pilaf

Burghul Mfalfal

برغل مغلغل

This dish is best served with yogurt (laban).

¼ **cup olive oil**
1 **cup medium bulgur**

½ **teaspoon salt**
¼ **teaspoon pepper**

2 **cups water**

Place the olive oil and bulgur in a saucepan, and sauté over medium-low heat for 4 minutes. Add the salt and pepper, and stir. Add the water and bring to a boil.

Turn the heat to low, cover, and simmer for 20 minutes, or until all the water is absorbed and the bulgur becomes fluffy. Stir gently. Serve warm.

Serves 3

Per serving: calories: 385, protein: 9 gm., carbohydrates: 47 gm., fat: 17 gm.

Cooked Chick-Peas
Hummus
حمص

1 cup dried chick-peas
4 cups water for cooking
¼ teaspoon baking soda

Cover the chick-peas with water, and soak overnight. Drain and place in a heavy pan. Add 4 cups fresh water and the baking soda. Cover and bring to a boil. Lower the heat and cook for 45 minutes or until the chick-peas are tender.

Makes 2 cups

Per cup: calories: 268, protein: 13 gm., carbohydrates: 46 gm., fat: 3 gm.

Cooked Rice
Riz Mfalfal
رز مغلفل

1 cup uncooked long grain white rice
¼ cup olive oil or canola oil

2 cups water
1 teaspoon salt

Heat the olive oil in a small pot. Rinse the rice in cold water several times, drain, and add to the olive oil. Sauté for 2 minutes.

Slowly and carefully add the water; it will sputter at first. Add the salt and bring to a boil. Cover and simmer over low heat for 15 minutes, or less if the water has evaporated. Stir once. Uncover and let set for 5 minutes before serving.

Serve with plain nonfat yogurt.

Serves 3

Per serving: calories: 317, protein: 3 gm., carbohydrates: 35 gm., fat: 14 gm.

Garlic Sauce
Salset Toom
ثوم

For the absolute garlic lovers!

6 cloves garlic, minced
¾ cup olive oil
¼ cup fresh lemon juice
salt to taste

Blend all the ingredients well.

Serve with broiled vegetables or any of your favorite recipes. You may want to add more lemon juice, to taste.

Makes approximately 1 cup

Per 2 Tablespoons: calories: 184, protein: 0 gm., carbohydrates: 2 gm., fat: 19 gm.

Pine Nut Sauce
Salset Al-Snawbar
صلصة الصنوبر

1 cup pine nuts
2 cloves garlic, minced
½ cup lemon juice
¼ teaspoon salt

¼ cup finely chopped fresh parsley

Combine all the ingredients, except the parsley, in a blender until smooth. Spoon into a bowl and garnish with the parsley.

You can use this sauce for vegetables, salads, or as a dip. You can adjust the amount of lemon juice to taste.

Makes 1½ cups

Per 2 Tablespoons: calories: 72, protein: 3 gm., carbohydrates: 3 gm., fat: 5 gm.

Tahini Sauce
Salset Tahini
طحينة

3 medium cloves garlic, minced
2½ teaspoons salt
1 cup tahini
1 cup water

1 cup fresh lemon juice
2 tablespoons red wine vinegar

Mix the garlic with the salt, then add the tahini. Add the water and mix gradually. Beat the mixture for 1 minute with a fork. Gradually add the lemon juice and vinegar, and blend well.

Makes approximately 2 cups

Per ¼ cup: calories: 200, protein: 5 gm., carbohydrates: 11 gm., fat: 15 gm.

Tahini Sauce with Parsley
Tarator
طرطور

This delicious sauce is commonly served on grilled fish. It also makes a healthful vegetable dip or a spread for sandwiches such as falafel.

3 medium cloves garlic, minced
2½ teaspoons salt
1 cup tahini
1 cup water

1 cup fresh lemon juice
1 cup chopped fresh green parsley
leaves

Mix the minced garlic with the salt, then add the tahini. Mix gradually as you add the water. Beat the mixture for 1 minute with a fork.

Gradually add the lemon juice, and blend well. Add the parsley and blend again.

Makes approximately 2 cups

Per ¼ cup: calories: 202, protein: 5 gm., carbohydrates: 11 gm., fat: 15 gm.

Yogurt
Laban
لبن

1 gallon whole milk
½ cup plain yogurt starter *rawbi*

Place the milk in a large heavy pot. Bring it to a gentle boil over low heat. Remove it from the stove, and let cool to luke-warm, about 115°F. The milk is ready when you can immerse your finger into it and count to ten comfortably. If the milk is too hot, wait longer; if it is too cool, return it to the heat and warm slightly.

Once ready, mix the yogurt starter (rawbi) with 8 tablespoons of the warm milk in a separate bowl. Blend together. Add to the rest of the milk, and stir well.

Place the pot on a kitchen counter, and cover with a lid. Wrap a blanket underneath and around the pot, and place another one on top. Leave undisturbed for 5 hours during the summer, or 6-8 hours if the weather is cooler.

Uncover and place the pot with the yogurt in the refrigerator. Once chilled, it is ready to be served or be made into Yogurt Spread (Labneh), page 41.

Makes 1 gallon
Per cup: calories: 155, protein: 9 gm., carbohydrates: 11 gm., fat: 7 gm.

Yogurt Sauce
Salset Al-Laban
صلصة اللبن

Great for the summer, this sauce can be used as a vegetable dip or as a spread for sandwiches.

2 medium cloves garlic, minced
salt to taste
¼ cup fresh green mint leaves,
   chopped, or 2 tablespoons dried mint
4 cups nonfat plain yogurt

1 cup water

Mix the garlic with the salt, mint, and yogurt. Gradually add the water and stir well.

Makes approximately 5 cups

Per cup: calories: 114, protein: 12 gm., carbohydrates: 16 gm., fat: 0 gm.

Appetizers

Mezza

مـازة

In Lebanon, the mezza is a very important component of the meal. It is a collection of small, authentic appetizer dishes served before the main course. A typical mezza consists of twenty to forty different dishes; the cold dishes are served first, followed by the hot dishes. A good mezza can last up to two hours, and some Lebanese people consider it the bulk of the meal. A large plate of freshly cut vegetables (lettuce, tomatoes, cucumbers, mint, parsley, radishes, green peppers, scallions, onions, etc.), as well as a bowl full of olives and pickled vegetables, is always in the center of the table.

Mezza is usually served with an anise-flavored drink called arak, made of sweet white grapes. Arak is very similar to the Greek drink, ouzu. It is served by pouring the arak in a small glass, filling it half way. Cold water and an ice cube are then added to fill up the glass.

Although a traditional mezza is most often served in restaurants, an abbreviated version is prepared in most Lebanese homes. The majority of dishes are vegetarian. Those that are not are usually prepared with lamb or fish.

In this section, we have included some of the vegetarian dishes most commonly served as part of the Lebanese mezza. Others are included in the salad, vegetable, legume, or stuffed vegetable sections. A list at the end of this section will indicate these recipes.

Bulgur with Eggplant
Burghul Bi-Batinjan
برغل بباتنجان

2 pounds eggplants

1 cup olive oil

3 white onions, chopped
3 cloves garlic, minced

4 cups water
2 cups medium bulgur

½ teaspoon cumin
½ teaspoon allspice
¾ teaspoon salt

Cut the eggplants into 3 x 2-inch pieces. Sprinkle with salt and soak in water for one hour, then drain and rinse well.

Heat the olive oil in a large skillet. Fry the eggplants until nearly brown on both sides. Remove and drain the excess oil on a paper towel. Fry the onions in the oil until golden, then add the garlic. Stir for 2 minutes. Remove and add to the eggplants.

Place the eggplants, onions, garlic, and water in a pot, and bring to a boil. Add the bulgur and seasonings. Make sure that there is enough water to barely cover the mixture. Simmer for 25 minutes or until the bulgur is tender and all the water has evaporated.

Serve cold with Yogurt in Mint Sauce (labneyeh) page 137. You can adjust the seasonings according to your taste. More water can be added while cooking the bulgur so that it will be tender when done.

Serves 5

Per serving: calories: 338, protein: 8 gm., carbohydrates: 52 gm., fat: 10 gm.

Chick-Pea Dip
Hummus-Bi-Tahini
دمص بطحينة

This ancient Lebanese/Middle Eastern dip has become a very popular vegetarian dish, served in countries around the world. It is best eaten with warm Arabic (pita) bread. Garbanzo beans and chick-peas are very similar. Either can be used for this recipe.

2 cups cooked, chick-peas, pg. 30
**½ cup reserved water from cooked
  chick-peas**
½ cup Tahini Sauce, pg. 32
½ cup fresh lemon juice
2 large cloves garlic, crushed
1 tablespoon salt

¼ cup extra-virgin olive oil
¼ teaspoon cayenne (red pepper)
2 tablespoons chopped fresh parsley

Place all the ingredients, except the olive oil, cayenne, and parsley, in a blender. Purée until smooth.

Spread the purée in a large, shallow plate. Sprinkle the olive oil on top, followed by the cayenne. Garnish with the parsley.

Serves 4
Per serving: calories: 454, protein: 11 gm., carbohydrates: 29 gm., fat: 33 gm.

Chick-Peas in Olive Oil
Msabahet Al-Hummus
مسبحة الحمص

This is one of our aunt Em-Kamal's favorite recipes. Not only does she serve it as part of the mezza, she also prepares it for morning brunch on Sundays. Adjust the amount of lemon juice to suit your taste.

2 cups cooked chick-peas

3 cloves garlic, minced
½ cup lemon juice
½ cup extra-virgin olive oil

1 tablespoon dried mint
salt to taste

Heat the cooked chick-peas and place in a salad bowl. Add the garlic, lemon juice, and olive oil, and mix well. Sprinkle in the mint and salt.

Serve right away with warm Arabic bread and a dish of your favorite vegetables. We like tomatoes, cucumbers, olives, green peppers, scallions, fresh green mint and parsley, and radishes.

Serves 4

Per serving: calories: 383, protein: 6 gm., carbohydrates: 26 gm., fat: 27 gm.

Eggplant in Tahini Sauce
Baba Ghanooj

بابا غنوج

"Baba" means daddy in Arabic. "Ghanooj" is a derivative of the verb "ghanaj" which generally means to spoil somebody. Why, where, or when this dish acquired its name is unknown. The year-round availability of eggplants in Lebanon makes this dish a very popular one. Recently, it has become a favorite in the vegetarian communities of many countries, including the United States. This dish can be prepared in several different ways, and we hope that you will enjoy our recipe. Feel free to adjust the amount of lemon juice to suit your taste.

3 medium eggplants

3 cloves garlic, minced
1 cup tahini
¼ cup water
1½ cups fresh lemon juice
salt to taste

⅛ cup extra-virgin olive oil
1 tablespoon chopped fresh green
  parsley

Remove the eggplant stems from the eggplants, and broil the eggplants, turning them regularly, until well done (approximately 20 minutes). Peel the skins off. Place the pulp in a food processor or blender, and blend well.

Mince the garlic with a pinch of salt. Add the tahini to the garlic, and mix well with the water and lemon juice. Add to the eggplant in the blender, and combine until smooth. Add salt to taste.

Spread the Baba Ghanooj in a large dish. Pour the olive oil over it, and garnish with the chopped parsley. Serve with tomato wedges, fresh radishes, and some juicy black olives.

Serves 5
Per serving: calories: 431, protein: 9 gm., carbohydrates: 38 gm., fat: 26 gm.

Pickled Turnips
Kabees al-lifit
كبيس

5 small turnips
1 small beet

¾ cup red wine vinegar
1½ cups water
¾ tablespoons salt

3 grape leaves or small cabbage leaves

Wash the turnips and beet well. Cut off the bottoms and tops, and slice ¼ inch thick. Combine the turnip and beet slices well in a mixing bowl, and pack into a 1-quart canning jar.

Mix the red wine vinegar with the water and salt. Pour the mixture into the canning jar until the turnips and beet are covered. Lay the grape leaves on top, and close the jar.

Set aside for at least 15 days. Once the jar is opened again, try to consume within 2 weeks or place in the refrigerator.

Makes 4 cups (8-10 servings)

Per serving: calories: 16, protein: 0 gm., carbohydrates: 4 gm., fat: 0 gm.

Yogurt Spread
Labneh-Bi-Zeyt
لبنة بزيت

There is no doubt that yogurt spread (labneh) is the most popular dish served in Lebanon today. In addition to being the principle dish for breakfast, it is also served as part of a mezza. In Lebanon yogurt is made from either sheep's or goat's milk.

In the United States, labneh is available in Lebanese food markets, Middle Eastern grocery stores, and some gourmet stores. We have included this quick, simple recipe to make your own labneh at home from prepared yogurt. However, should you prefer to do it from scratch, follow the guidelines for making yogurt (laban) on page 33.

2 quarts plain yogurt
2 teaspoons salt

Pour the yogurt into a tightly woven, unbleached muslin cloth, place over a strainer, and let it drain for a day at room temperature. When there is no more liquid draining from the bag, remove the yogurt and place in a bowl. Add the salt and mix well. Refrigerate overnight in a covered glass container.

Serve for breakfast, dinner, or as part of a mezza. Spread the dry yogurt (labneh) in a shallow plate, and sprinkle extra-virgin olive oil and dried mint on top. Add a few green or black olives, and enjoy with warm pita bread.

Makes 2 cups

Per ½ cup: calories: 309, protein: 18 gm., carbohydrates: 23 gm., fat: 16 gm.

Yogurt Spread Cheese Balls in Olive Oil
Labneh Mkabtaleh Makbuseh
لبنة مكبتلة مكبوسة

This version of labneh is most often prepared in the mountains of Lebanon. This is a great way of preserving the labneh for a very long time.

2 cups Yogurt Spread (labneh), pg. 41
1 cup extra-virgin olive oil

Roll the labneh into small balls the size of golf balls. Place in a sterilized glass jar, and chill overnight.

The following morning, add enough of the olive oil to cover, and seal the jar. Store at room temperature in a dark cabinet. Once opened, it can be kept in the refrigerator for one week.

You can add any flavorful herb you like, such as rosemary, oregano, or thyme, to the jar of labneh balls to add flavor.

Makes 10 balls

Per ball: calories: 219, protein: 7 gm., carbohydrates: 9 gm., fat: 17 gm.

Yogurt Spread with Garlic
Labneh-Bi-Toom
لبنة بثوم

Similar to labneh, this version is for the garlic lover!

2 cups Yogurt Spread (labneh), pg. 41
2 large cloves garlic, minced
¼ teaspoon salt

Place the labneh in a bowl, and mix with the garlic and salt. Cover and refrigerate overnight to allow the garlic to flavor the labneh.

Spread the labneh in a shallow plate. Serve with cut cucumbers, tomatoes, and fresh mint leaves, and eat with pita bread.

Makes 2 cups

Per ½ cup: calories: 309, protein: 18 gm., carbohydrates: 23 gm., fat: 16 gm.

Other Mezza Recipes

In addition to the recipes in this section, there are a number of recipes which appear in other sections of this book that could be served as part of a mezza. You'll find them on the pages indicated after the recipe title.

Soups
Shorbat
شوربة

In Lebanon, soups are most commonly prepared during the winter season. Although many of them use animal broth as a base and chunks of lamb or chicken, several soups are traditionally vegetarian. Vegetables that are not fresh enough for a good salad are very useful in many of the soups. There is no need to waste any vegetables! Grains such as lentils and beans are commonly used. In this section, we have included a few of our favorite soup recipes. We hope that you will enjoy them.

Lentils and Swiss Chard Soup
Shorbat Adas Bi-Silek
شوربة عدس بسلق

1 cup whole lentils
2 quarts cold water

2 medium potatoes, diced
1 bunch Swiss chard, coarsely
  chopped

2 medium onions, chopped
½ cup olive oil
6 cloves garlic, crushed
⅛ cup white flour dissolved in ¼ cup
  cold water

½ cup fresh lemon juice
salt to taste

Wash the lentils well. Place in a soup pot, and cover with the water. Cover the pot and cook until half done (approximately 20 minutes).

Add the potatoes and Swiss chard. Cover again and cook for about 25 minutes.

Meanwhile, in a sauté pan, sauté the onions in the olive oil until brown. Add the garlic and sauté for 3 more minutes. Add the flour mixture, stir well, and bring to a boil. Add the onion mixture to the lentils and vegetables, cover, and cook for 10 more minutes. Add the lemon juice, salt, and stir well.

Serve warm or cold in soup bowls. More lemon juice may be added at the end of the cooking time to add more flavor.

Serves 6

Per serving: calories: 347, protein: 9 gm., carbohydrates: 37 gm., fat: 17 gm.

Lentil-Noodle Soup
Richta Bi-Adas
رشطة بعدس

2 cups whole lentils
8 cups water

3 large onions, finely chopped
5 cloves garlic, crushed
1 pound Swiss chard, chopped
½ cup olive oil

1 cup uncooked wide or thin noodles
2 bunches fresh green cilantro, finely chopped
salt and pepper to taste

Place the lentils in a large pot, and cover with water. Cook over medium heat until done (about 25 minutes), but not to the point where the lentils are mushy.

Sauté the vegetables in the olive oil until lightly brown, and add to the lentils. Cook over medium heat until the vegetables are tender.

Add the noodles and seasonings. Cook for 20 minutes, or until the noodles are tender.

Serve hot in wide soup bowls garnished with lemon wedges.

Serves 6
Per serving: calories: 430, protein: 15 gm., carbohydrates: 51 gm., fat: 17 gm.

Lentil Soup with Olive Oil
Shorbat Bi-Zeyt Zeytoon
شوربة بزيت زيتون

1 cup whole lentils
6 cups water
½ cup uncooked white rice

1 large onion, coarsely chopped
½ cup olive oil
salt and pepper to taste

¼ cup finely chopped fresh parsley

Rinse the lentils and drain. Cover with the water and cook in a medium pot for 20 minutes, or until the lentils are tender. Add the rice.

Sauté the onions in the olive oil until golden, and add to the lentil mixture, along with all the olive oil remaining in the pan. Cook for 15 more minutes. Add the salt and pepper, then cook for 5 more minutes.

Garnish with the parsley and serve warm in soup bowls.

Variation: You can add ¼ teaspoon of cumin along with the salt and pepper.

Serves 3

Per serving: calories: 517, protein: 11 gm., carbohydrates: 37 gm., fat: 34 gm.

Southern Lentil Soup
Shorbat Mamrouteh
شوربة ممروطة

A delicious soup from the mountains of southern Lebanon. This is our dad's favorite soup. It is best served hot on a cold winter day.

2 cups whole lentils

1 large onion, chopped
½ cup olive oil

½ cup uncooked white rice

¼ cup fresh lemon juice
1 cup chopped parsley leaves
1 tablespoon ground cumin
salt and black pepper to taste

2 Arabic breads, cut in 1-inch pieces

Rinse the lentils in cold water, drain, and place in a medium pot. Cover with water and cook until tender, about 20 minutes.

Meanwhile, sauté the onions in the olive oil, and set aside. Remove the lentils from the pot, and either purée in a food processor or press through a sieve. Return the puréed lentils to the pot, and add the rice and onions. Bring to a boil, lower the heat, and simmer until the soup is thickened. Add water as needed.

Just before serving, add the lemon juice, parsley, cumin, salt, and pepper, and mix. Serve with toasted pieces of Arabic bread.

Serves 6-8

Per serving: calories: 313, protein: 9 gm., carbohydrates: 33 gm., fat: 15 gm.

Spinach Lentil Soup
Shorbat Sbanegh Bi-Adas
شوربة سبانغ بعدس

1 cup whole lentils
4 cups water

2 teaspoons salt
¾ cup finely diced red potatoes
2 cups finely chopped fresh spinach

1 cup finely chopped onion
½ cup olive oil
6 large cloves garlic, minced

¼ cup lemon juice

Rinse the lentils and drain. Cook the lentils in the water in a medium pot until almost tender, about 20 minutes.

Add the salt, potatoes, and spinach.

Sauté the onions in the olive oil in a separate pan until limp. Add half the garlic to the onion, and stir well. Sauté until golden brown.

Add the onion to the lentils, and bring to a boil while stirring well. Lower the heat and cook for 20 more minutes. Add the lemon juice and the rest of the garlic just before serving, and stir well. Serve hot or cold.

Variation: Sauté ½ cup chopped fresh cilantro along with the garlic and onions.

Serves 4-6

Per serving: calories: 352, protein: 8 gm., carbohydrates: 32 gm., fat: 21 gm.

Salads
Salata
صلطة

Armenian Cucumber Salad
Salatet El-Mekta
صلطة المقتى

"Mekta" is called Armenian cucumber in the United States. It is mostly grown in the summertime in Lebanon and is also available in parts of the United States in the summer.

3 small tomatoes, cut into ½-inch cubes
3 small Armenian cucumbers, sliced

2 tablespoons red wine vinegar
juice of 1 lemon
2 tablespoons extra-virgin olive oil
1 teaspoon dried mint

Combine the tomatoes and cucumbers in a medium salad bowl.

Pour the vinegar, lemon juice, olive oil, and mint over them, and mix well.

Chill for 2 hours and serve.

Serves 2

Per serving: calories: 220, protein: 3 gm., carbohydrates: 20 gm., fat: 13 gm.

Artichoke Salad
Salatet Ardichaouki
صلطة أرضي شوكة

2 cloves garlic, minced
½ teaspoon salt
¼ cup fresh lemon juice
¼ cup extra-virgin olive oil

4 medium fresh artichokes

2 teaspoons fresh lemon juice
1 teaspoon flour
1 cup boiling water

2 teaspoons chopped fresh parsley

To make the dressing, mix the garlic, salt, lemon juice, and olive oil in a salad bowl.

Cut off the artichokes stems, and break off the outside leaves. Remove all of the fuzzy choke with a teaspoon, and cut out the inside leaves. Rinse the artichokes several times with cold water.

Soak the artichokes for 15 minutes in enough water to cover mixed with the 2 teaspoons fresh lemon juice and the flour.

Drain the artichokes, place in a saucepan, and add 1 cup boiling water. Cook in boiling water for 15 minutes, or until the artichokes are tender. Drain and mix with the dressing while still hot.

Garnish with the parsley and serve cold.

Serves 2-4
Per serving: calories: 239, protein: 2 gm., carbohydrates: 17 gm., fat: 17 gm.

Bean Salad
Salatet Al-Fasoolia

صلطة الفاصولية

1 cup cooked chick-peas
1 cup cooked lima beans
1 cup cooked kidney beans
1 medium red onion, thinly sliced

Dressing:
2 cloves garlic, crushed
1 teaspoon salt
⅓ cup fresh lemon juice
⅓ cup extra-virgin olive oil
¼ teaspoon black pepper

½ cup finely chopped fresh green
  parsley

Mix the chick-peas, lima beans, kidney beans, and onion in a large bowl.

Combine the dressing ingredients and pour over the beans. Add the parsley.

Toss gently and place in the refrigerator for at least 2 hours before serving.

Serves 6

Per serving: calories: 235, protein: 7 gm., carbohydrates: 25 gm., fat: 11 gm.

Beet Salad
Salatet Al-Shamandar
سلطة الشمندر

1 pound beets, cooked and thinly sliced
1 small white onion, thinly sliced
⅓ cup red wine vinegar
⅓ cup extra-virgin olive oil
1 teaspoon salt

½ cup coarsely chopped fresh parsley

Combine the beets, onion, vinegar, olive oil, and salt, and mix well.

Garnish with the parsley.

You can serve right away or refrigerate for later use.

Serves 4

Per serving: calories: 196, protein: 1 gm., carbohydrates: 10 gm., fat: 15 gm.

55

Bulgur-Parsley Salad
Tabouli
تبولة

Although Lebanese people seldom agree on any issue, they all agree that tabouli is their favorite salad! This dish is served as part of the mezza, as a main course, or as a mid-afternoon dish on a hot summer day. It is another Lebanese dish which is becoming more and more popular in vegetarian circles around the world. Although a little chopping is needed, it is really worth the effort.

As you will soon discover, the principle ingredient of tabouli is parsley. Parsley is an herb with a variety of health related benefits (see page 18).

½ cup medium bulgur, washed and
  drained
¾ cup fresh lemon juice

4 bunches parsley, cleaned, washed,
  and finely chopped
4 medium tomatoes, finely chopped
1 bunch scallions, chopped
1 cup finely chopped fresh mint
1 small white onion, finely chopped

¾ cup extra-virgin olive oil
1 tablespoon salt
1 teaspoon allspice

1 head romaine lettuce, washed and
  separated into leaves

Combine ½ cup boiling water with the bulgur in a small bowl; cover and let sit for 15 minutes. Squeeze the excess water out. Pour the lemon juice over the bulgur, and let stand at room temperature for 5 minutes.

Mix all the vegetables and add to the bulgur. Add the olive oil, salt, and allspice, and mix thoroughly with the vegetables.

Serve the tabouli by filling each lettuce leaf in the center and eating it like a taco.

Serves 6
Per serving: calories: 293, protein: 2 gm., carbohydrates: 11 gm., fat: 26 gm.

Cabbage and Tomato Salad
Salatet Malfoof Bi-Banadoora
صلطة ملفوف ببندورة

1 small head white cabbage, finely shredded

juice of 2 small lemons
3 cloves garlic, crushed
3 tablespoons extra-virgin olive oil
salt to taste

3 medium tomatoes, finely diced

If you like, you can soak the cabbage in ice water, and let it set for an hour. Drain well and squeeze out the excess water. The ice makes the cabbage crunchy and gives it a good flavor.

Mix the lemon juice, garlic, olive oil, and salt. Pour over the cabbage, add the tomatoes, and mix well.

Refrigerate for 30 minutes, then serve with lentils and rice.

Serves 4

Per serving: calories: 130, protein: 1 gm., carbohydrates: 9 gm., fat: 9 gm.

Cucumber and Tomato Salad
Salatet Khiar Bi-Banadoora
صلطة خيار ببندورة

2 cloves garlic, minced
½ teaspoon salt

juice of 1 large lemon

1 large tomato, cut into ½-inch cubes
1 large cucumber, peeled and thinly
  sliced

2 tablespoons extra-virgin olive oil
2 tablespoons red wine vinegar

½ cup finely chopped fresh parsley
1 tablespoon chopped white onion
  (optional)

In a medium salad bowl, mix the garlic and salt. Add the lemon juice and mix well.

Add the tomato and cucumber to the garlic, and mix again.

Add the olive oil and vinegar, mix again, and sprinkle with the parsley and onion.

Serves 2-4

58   Per serving: calories: 110, protein: 1 gm., carbohydrates: 6 gm., fat: 9 gm.

Cucumber and Yogurt Salad
Salatet Khiar–Bi–Laban
صلطة خيار بلبن

A very refreshing salad served on hot days in Lebanon.

2 large cloves garlic, minced
1½ teaspoons salt
1 quart nonfat plain yogurt
½ cup cold water

2 small cucumbers, peeled and diced
1½ tablespoons dried mint, or 10 leaves fresh mint, coarsely chopped

Mix the garlic with the salt. Add to the yogurt and water, and blend well.

Toss the cucumbers and mint together. Pour the yogurt mixture over the cucumbers, and blend well.

Chill for 2-3 hours, then serve.

Serves 4

Per serving: calories: 152, protein: 16 gm., carbohydrates: 21 gm., fat: 0 gm.

Eggplant Salad
Salatet Al-Batinjan

سلطة الباتنجان

1 medium eggplant

2 scallions, finely chopped

1 medium clove garlic, minced
½ teaspoon salt
⅛ teaspoon black pepper
¼ cup fresh lemon juice
2 tablespoons olive oil

1 tablespoon finely chopped fresh
  parsley

Broil the eggplant for 20 minutes, turning it regularly. Remove and run under cold water to loosen the skin. Peel and cut into 1-inch pieces.

Place the eggplants in a salad bowl, and add the scallions. Set aside.

Mix the garlic, salt, pepper, lemon juice, and olive oil. Pour over the eggplant and mix well.

Garnish with parsley and serve.

Serves 2

Per serving: calories: 204, protein: 1 gm., carbohydrates: 20 gm., fat: 13 gm.

Fava Bean Salad
Salatet Al-Fasoolia
صلطة الفاصولية

1 cup green fava beans

1 small white onion, finely chopped
⅓ cup fresh lemon juice
1 tablespoon white wine vinegar
1 teaspoon salt
¼ cup extra-virgin olive oil

1 tablespoon coarsely chopped parsley

Place the fava beans in a saucepan, and add enough water to cover. Bring to a boil, reduce the heat to medium, and cook until tender.

Drain the water and add the onion, lemon juice, vinegar, and salt. Stir well. Add the olive oil and gently mix. Garnish with the parsley and serve.

Serves 4
Per serving: calories: 182, protein: 3 gm., carbohydrates: 12 gm., fat: 13 gm.

Green Bean Salad
Loobeye Mutabali

لوبية متبلة

1½ pounds fresh green beans

3 small cloves garlic, minced
½ cup fresh lemon juice
½ cup extra-virgin olive oil
½ teaspoon salt

Trim the ends off the green beans, and wash in cold water. Break into 2-inch pieces. Cook in salted water until tender. Drain and cool.

Mix the garlic, lemon juice, olive oil, and salt. Pour over the green beans, and toss well.

Serves 4-6

Per serving: calories: 241, protein: 2 gm., carbohydrates: 11 gm., fat: 21 gm.

Lebanese Vegetable Salad
Fattoosh
فتوش

Fattoosh is a specialty salad served in Lebanese homes at least once a week. Instead of discarding small pieces of Arabic bread after each meal, they are saved. When enough bread is gathered, a fattoosh is assembled!

3 tablespoons olive oil
Equivalent of 1½ loaves Arabic bread, toasted and cut into 1-inch squares

1 large cucumber, peeled and diced
3 medium tomatoes, cut into 1-inch cubes
½ bunch romaine lettuce, finely chopped
½ cup coarsely chopped fresh parsley leaves
6 scallions, finely sliced
½ medium green pepper, cut into ½-inch squares
4 large radishes, cut into 1-inch cubes
2 tablespoons chopped fresh mint

Dressing:
2 large cloves garlic, minced
½ cup fresh lemon juice
2 tablespoons red wine vinegar
⅓ cup extra-virgin olive oil
1 tablespoon salt

In a large pan, heat the 3 tablespoons of olive oil, and sauté the toasted bread until golden brown. Remove and set aside.

In a large salad bowl, mix all the vegetables well.

Mix the dressing ingredients. Add half of the dressing to the vegetables, and mix well. Add the sautéed bread and the other half of the dressing to the vegetables, and mix again.

This salad must be served right away, as letting it set overnight would spoil the texture of the sautéed bread. It can be served by itself or as part of a mezza.

Serves 6
Per serving: calories: 270, protein: 3 gm., carbohydrates: 23 gm., fat: 17 gm.

Potato Salad
Salatet Al-Batata
صلطة البطاطا

The smell of wild, green thyme covers the hills of Lebanon, especially in the south in late spring and summer. This herb is known to have many health benefits (see page 18).

**2 pounds white potatoes, boiled and
  cut into ½-inch cubes**
1 large tomato, diced

**1 small white onion, chopped, or
  1 bunch scallions, chopped**
1 tablespoon fresh thyme leaves
1 tablespoon chopped fresh parsley
1 teaspoon ground cumin (optional)
¼ cup fresh lemon juice
1 tablespoon extra-virgin olive oil
1 teaspoon salt

Mix the potatoes with the tomatoes. Add the onion, thyme, parsley, cumin, lemon juice, olive oil, and salt. Toss and serve.

Variation: More lemon juice can be used depending on your personal taste.

Serves 6

Per serving: calories: 159, protein: 2 gm., carbohydrates: 33 gm., fat: 2 gm.

Spinach Salad
Salatet Al-Sbanegh
صلطة السبانخ

1 bunch spinach, well washed and coarsely chopped
1 teaspoon salt

1 small white onion, chopped
1 medium tomato, diced

¼ cup extra-virgin olive oil
¼ cup fresh lemon juice
½ teaspoon allspice

Place the spinach in a salad bowl. Sprinkle with the salt and rub the spinach with your fingers. Squeeze out the excess water, and drain.

Add the onions and tomatoes.

Mix the olive oil, lemon juice, and spices well, and pour over the vegetables. Toss well and serve.

Variation: A dash of Middle Eastern sumac can be added with the spices.

Serves 4
Per serving: calories: 144, protein: 1 gm., carbohydrates: 4 gm., fat: 13 gm.

Thyme Salad
Salatet Al-Zaatar
صلطة الزعتر

This salad may be used as an appetizer.

1 cup fresh thyme leaves

1 small white onion, finely chopped
1 teaspoon salt

¼ cup lemon juice
½ cup extra-virgin olive oil

Pick off the thyme leaves, and discard the stems. Rinse the leaves in cold water, drain well, and set aside.

Mix the onion with ½ teaspoon of the salt. Add the thyme leaves to the onion, and mix with the lemon juice, olive oil, and the remaining salt.

Serve with Arabic bread.

Serves 3-4

Per serving: calories: 280, protein: 0 gm., carbohydrates: 2 gm., fat: 29 gm.

Tomato Salad
Salatet Al-Banadoora
صلطة البندورة

This salad is usually served with Lentils with Bulgur (Moujadara Bi-Burghul), page 107, or as part of a mezza.

2 cloves garlic, crushed
¼ to ½ cup fresh lemon juice
2 teaspoons salt

3 medium tomatoes, cut into small wedges
2 scallions, coarsely chopped (optional)
10 fresh green mint leaves, coarsely chopped, or 1 tablespoon dried mint

¼ cup extra-virgin olive oil

Mix the garlic, lemon juice, and salt.

Add to the vegetables and mint, and toss well. Add the olive oil and toss again gently.

Variation: You can add ½ cup of sliced, cooked beets to this salad to enhance its color.

Serves 4

Per serving: calories: 145, protein: 1 gm., carbohydrates: 6 gm., fat: 13 gm.

Zucchini Salad
Salatet Al-Koosa
صلطة الكوسى

2 pounds zucchini or summer squash,
  cut into 1-inch discs
1 cup olive oil

juice of 2 lemons
1 teaspoon red wine vinegar
2 tablespoons dried mint
salt to taste

Sauté the zucchini or squash in the olive oil until golden. Place on a paper towel to drain.

Place the zucchini or squash in a salad bowl, and add the lemon juice and vinegar. Sprinkle with the mint and salt, and adjust the seasoning, if needed.

Serve cold.

Serves 4

Per serving: calories: 154, protein: 2 gm., carbohydrates: 7 gm., fat: 13 gm.

Vegetables

Khodar

خضار

Cilantro Green Beans
Loobeye Bi-Kizbara
لوبية بكزبرة

6 cups fresh string beans

¼ cup olive oil
1 medium red onion, chopped

3 cups fresh cilantro leaves
¼ cup water

8 cloves garlic, peeled and diced
½ teaspoon salt

Trim the ends of the string beans, and chop into 2-inch pieces.

Heat the olive oil in a large pot. Add the onion and sauté over high heat for 4 minutes. Add the beans to the onion, and sauté for 15 minutes over medium-high heat, stirring often.

Wash the cilantro and pick off the leaves. Chop the leaves and add to the pot along with the ¼ cup water. Cook for 10 more minutes, stirring often.

Add the garlic and cook for 4 more minutes over medium heat. Once done, add the salt and mix well. You can serve this warm or cold.

Serves 3

Per serving: calories: 246, protein: 4 gm., carbohydrates: 21 gm., fat: 17 gm.

Dandelions with Onions
Hindbeh Bi-Zeyt
هندبة بزيت

Dandelions contain a range of vitamins and minerals and have health enhancing properties (see page 18). In Lebanon, dandelions are sold in farmers' markets year round. The Lebanese love this green vegetable because it's delicious and nutritious. This dish is Dalal's favorite!

3 quarts water
1½ pounds tender dandelions,
  cleaned, washed, and finely chopped

3 large white onions, julienned
½ cup olive oil
1 clove garlic, minced with ¼
  teaspoon salt

lemon juice to taste
salt to taste

Bring the water to a boil, and add the dandelions and a pinch of salt. Cover and simmer for 20 minutes, or until the dandelions are tender. Drain and squeeze out the excess water.

Sauté the onions in the olive oil until golden brown. Set aside half the onions. Add the garlic and salt, and sauté for 2 minutes. Add the dandelions and sauté for 5 more minutes, stirring often.

Remove and put on a large, shallow plate. Garnish with the other half of the onions. Sprinkle on lemon juice and salt to taste.

Serve right away with warm pita bread and lemon wedges.

Serves 4
Per serving: calories: 385, protein: 5 gm., carbohydrates: 24 gm., fat: 33 gm.

Green Bean Stew
Loobeye Bi-Zeyt
لوبية بزيت

2 pounds fresh green beans

1 medium onion, chopped
5 large cloves garlic, minced
½ cup extra-virgin olive oil

1 cup water
2 medium ripe whole tomatoes, peeled
and diced
1 cup tomato sauce

salt and pepper to taste

Trim the ends and remove the strings from the green beans. Wash, cut into 3-inch pieces, and set aside.

Sauté the onion and garlic in the olive oil. Add the beans and sauté for a couple of minutes. Cover and steam in their own juice for 15 minutes.

Add the 1 cup water, tomatoes, and tomato sauce, cover, and cook for 30 more minutes over low heat.

Season to taste with salt and pepper.

Serves 4

Per serving: calories: 372, protein: 4 gm., carbohydrates: 24 gm., fat: 33 gm.

Green Pepper with Tomatoes
Shakshoukeh
شكشوكة

This dish can be used as a sauce if the green pepper is omitted and all other ingredients are doubled.

3 medium green peppers, diced
¼ cup olive oil

3 large ripe tomatoes, diced
8 cloves garlic, minced
2 tablespoons ground coriander
½ teaspoon salt

Sauté the green peppers in the olive oil until limp. Add the tomatoes and sauté for 5 minutes. Add the garlic, coriander, and salt, and mix well. Cover and cook for 3 more minutes.

Serve cold with pita bread.

Serves 4-6

Per serving: calories: 134, protein: 1 gm., carbohydrates: 7 gm., fat: 16 gm.

Lebanese Okra
Bemya
بميــة

When cooked correctly, okra can be a heavenly dish. When picking okra at the food market, choose ones that are small and green. Avoid those that are stained, brown, and sticky. This dish is best served with rice such as Lebanese Rice (Riz Bi-Sheereeyee), page 111. Sprinkle a few teaspoons of freshly squeezed lemon juice on top, and you are in heaven!

4 cups okra
½ cup olive oil

5 small white onions, chopped
5 small, ripe tomatoes, chopped

2 cloves garlic, sliced
1 tablespoon salt
1½ cups fresh cilantro leaves, finely chopped

Cut the stems off the okra, and wash a few times in cold water. In a large pot, heat 3 tablespoons of the olive oil, and sauté the okra over medium-high heat until brown. Remove and set aside.

Put the onions in the pot, and add 3 more tablespoons of the olive oil. Sauté for 5 minutes and then add the tomatoes. Cook for 5 more minutes.

Add the okra, remaining olive oil, garlic, salt, and coriander. Sauté for 3 more minutes over high heat, stirring frequently.

Add enough water to barely cover the contents of the pot. Bring to a boil, then reduce the heat to medium. Cook partially covered until all the water has evaporated.

This dish can be served hot or cold as desired, accompanied with warm pita bread.

Serves 4

Per serving: calories: 318, protein: 3 gm., carbohydrates: 16 gm., fat: 26 gm.

The Maalouf Family's Puréed Potatoes
Al Maalouf Kibbit Al-Batata
ال معلوف كبة الباطاطا

This is another version of Potato Casserole (Kibbit al-Batata), page 79. While working on this book, a friend of Maher's, Dr. Nadim Maalouf, told him that his mother and grandmother have their own delicious version of this recipe which they cook in their Bekaa valley town of Niha. We are delighted to include this recipe and give credit to Mrs. Nabiha Maalouf and Mrs. Samira Maalouf.

1½ cups medium bulgur
3 large white potatoes

1 medium white onion, cut into large pieces

3 cloves garlic, minced
1 cup tahini
juice of 3 lemons
3 tablespoons olive oil
1 teaspoon salt

fresh mint and scallions for decoration

Soak the bulgur in hot water for 30 minutes. Meanwhile, boil the potatoes until tender. Peel the potatoes and purée in a food processor, then remove. Put the onion in the food processor, and finely chop (avoid turning the onions into juice).

Combine the onions with the potatoes and bulgur in a large bowl. Add the garlic and mix well. Add the tahini, lemon juice, and olive oil; mix well again. Sprinkle on the salt and serve.

Spread the puréed potatoes on a large, shallow plate, and garnish with mint and scallions. Serve with warm pita bread.

Serves 6

Per serving: calories: 499, protein: 12 gm., carbohydrates: 51 gm., fat: 27 gm.

Potatoes in Tahini Sauce
Batata Bi-Tahini
بطاطا بطحينة

Small red potatoes are best suited for this delicious recipe.

Tahini Sauce:
1 cup tahini
3 cloves garlic, crushed
3½ cups fresh lemon juice
3 tablespoons cold water

6 large red potatoes, boiled, peeled,
  and cut into 2-inch cubes
salt and pepper to taste
½ cup chopped fresh parsley

Prepare the tahini sauce by mixing the tahini with the garlic, lemon juice, and water and beating continuously with a spoon until it becomes creamy and smooth.

Pour the sauce over the potatoes, add salt and pepper, and garnish with the parsley. Serve immediately or marinate longer to bring out the flavor.

Serves 6-8

Per serving: calories: 352, protein: 7 gm., carbohydrates: 41 gm., fat: 18 gm.

Potatoes with Cilantro
Batata Bi-Kizbara
بطاطا بكزبرة

Sautéing fresh cilantro (coriander) with garlic in olive oil produces an irresistible aroma. It is one of Maher's favorite childhood kitchen memories.

½ cup olive oil or canola oil
6 medium potatoes, peeled and cut into 1-inch cubes

1 cup coarsely chopped fresh cilantro leaves
8 large cloves garlic, crushed
salt to taste
½ teaspoon red pepper (cayenne)

Heat the olive oil in a large, deep pan, and sauté the potatoes until golden brown. Remove and place on a paper towel to drain the excess oil.

Sauté the cilantro and garlic in the olive oil in a separate frying pan. Add the potatoes, season with the salt and red pepper, stir well, and serve warm with pita bread.

Serves 6
Per serving: calories: 281, protein: 2 gm., carbohydrates: 29 gm., fat: 16 gm.

Sautéed Green Beans
Loobeye Mekleeyee
لوبية مقلية

This dish is best served with a side dish of rice.

⅓ cup olive oil
2 medium white onions, finely chopped

1½ pounds fresh green beans

1 teaspoon salt
½ teaspoon cumin
½ teaspoon allspice

9 scallions, chopped into ½-inch pieces
juice of 2 lemons

Heat the olive oil in a large pot. Add the onions and sauté until light golden in color.

Trim the green beans and chop into 1-inch pieces. Add to the onions and sauté for another 15 minutes on medium heat, stirring often.

Add 3 cups of hot water to the beans, and bring to a boil. Reduce the heat to medium-low, cover, and cook for 25 minutes. Once done, drain the excess water.

Add the salt, cumin, and allspice to the beans, and mix well. Divide among 4 large, shallow plates, and cover with the scallions. Pour the lemon juice over, and serve hot or cold, as desired.

Serves 4

Per serving: calories: 240, protein: 3 gm., carbohydrates: 16 gm., fat: 20 gm.

Potato Casserole
Kibbit Al-Batata
كبة البطاطا

1½ pounds red potatoes

2 medium white onions, finely chopped
3 cloves garlic, minced
1 bunch fresh green cilantro leaves, chopped
½ cup olive oil

1 cup medium bulgur, soaked in ½ cup boiling water for 10 minutes
½ teaspoon white pepper
½ teaspoon nutmeg
½ teaspoon cumin
½ teaspoon black pepper
½ cup flour

Boil the whole potatoes until tender.

Meanwhile, sauté the onions, garlic, and cilantro in ¼ cup of the olive oil until golden.

Peel the potatoes when done, and place in a food processor or blender. Mash and mix with the soaked bulgur, seasonings, and flour, and place in a casserole dish.

Preheat the oven to 350°F.

Sprinkle on the remainder of the olive oil, and bake in the oven for 30 minutes.

Serves 4-6
Per serving: calories: 450, protein: 6 gm., carbohydrates: 58 gm., fat: 21 gm.

Swiss Chard in Tahini Sauce
Mtabel Al-Silek
متبل السلق

Mtabel Al-silek is a good dish for using up the ribs of Swiss chard leftover from recipes where only the leaves are used. It can be eaten as a dish with Stuffed Chard (Mihshi Waraq Silek), page 88, or used as a vegetable dip.

1 cup water
2 cups Swiss chard ribs, cut into
  2-inch pieces

½ cup tahini
2 medium cloves garlic, minced
½ cup fresh lemon juice
1 teaspoon salt

2 teaspoons finely chopped fresh
  green parsley, for garnish
3 tablespoons extra-virgin olive oil

Bring the water to a boil in a medium pot, and add the Swiss chard ribs. Cover and simmer for 10 minutes. Remove the ribs and drain well.

Place the ribs in a food processor, and finely chop. Add the tahini, garlic, lemon juice, and salt, and blend well.

Spread the blended mixture (silek) on a large, shallow plate, and garnish with the parsley. Sprinkle with the olive oil, and serve cold.

Serves 3

80   Per serving: calories: 247, protein: 7 gm., carbohydrates: 15 gm., fat: 21 gm.

Vegetable Stew
Siniyet Al-Khodar Makhloota
صنية الخضار مخلوطة

This is Dalal's famous stew—her children's and neighbor's favorite! Give it a try.

1 large eggplant, peeled and cut into 2-inch pieces

4 large potatoes, cut into 2-inch cubes
1½ cups canola oil
2 large zucchini, cut into 2-inch cubes

2 large carrots, thinly sliced
1 large onion, julienned
6 cloves garlic, minced

1 teaspoon cinnamon
1 teaspoon black pepper
2 teaspoons salt

4 large ripe tomatoes, peeled, seeded, and diced
1 cup water

Soak the eggplant pieces in a large bowl of water mixed with 1 teaspoon salt.

Meanwhile, fry the potatoes in the canola oil until golden brown. Remove and set aside. Add the zucchini to the oil, and fry for a few minutes, until light golden. Do not brown! Remove and add to the potatoes.

In a separate pan, add 1 tablespoon of the hot oil, and sauté the carrots until limp. Remove. Sauté the onion until golden, and add the garlic 1 minute before the onion is done. Remove.

Preheat the oven to 350°F. Drain the eggplant and fry in the canola oil until golden brown. Remove and add to all the vegetables in a large baking pan. Add the seasonings and mix well. Place the tomatoes on top of the vegetables, and pour the water over all. Cover with aluminum foil and bake for 30-45 minutes. The stew is done when all the vegetables are tender.

You can serve this hot or cold. It tastes great with warm pita bread.

Serves 6-8

Per serving: calories: 331, protein: 2 gm., carbohydrates: 29 gm., fat: 23 gm.

From the Tables of Lebanon

Stuffed Vegetables
Mihshi
محشي

Stuffed Artichokes
Ardichaouki Mihsheeyee

أرضي شوكة محشية

8 small fresh artichokes
4 quarts cold water
1 tablespoon flour
4 lemon wedges

1 cup diced carrots
1 cup boiling water
1 cup frozen peas

¼ cup canola oil
½ cup chopped white onions

2 cups water
¼ teaspoon black pepper

3 large cloves garlic
½ cup fresh lemon juice
½ teaspoon salt
¼ cup olive oil

Wash the artichokes well. Cut off the outer artichoke leaves, and cut the stems so the artichokes will have a flat base to sit on. (If the artichokes won't sit up, dig out more of the stem end with the tip of a knife.) Cut through the upper third of the artichokes to expose the fuzzy choke. Scoop out the choke with a teaspoon, and trim off the bottom row of leaves. Place the artichokes in a large bowl, and combine with the water, flour, and lemon wedges. Soak the artichokes in this mixture for at least 15 minutes.

Add the carrots to 1 cup of boiling water, and simmer for 5 minutes. Add the peas and simmer for another 5 minutes. Drain and set aside.

Fry the artichokes in the canola oil until golden brown, remove, and set aside. Add the onions to the oil, and fry until limp. Remove, add to the carrots and peas, and mix well.

Stuff the inside of the artichokes with the carrots, peas, and onions. Arrange the stuffed artichokes in a shallow casserole dish. Place any extra carrots, peas, and onions between the artichokes. Cover with the 2 cups water, and top with the black pepper. Cook at 350°F for 30 minutes.

Serves 6

Per serving: calories: 285, protein: 4 gm., carbohydrates: 25 gm., fat: 20 gm.

When done, mix the garlic, lemon juice, salt, and olive oil. Pour over the artichokes. Let set for a few minutes, then serve.

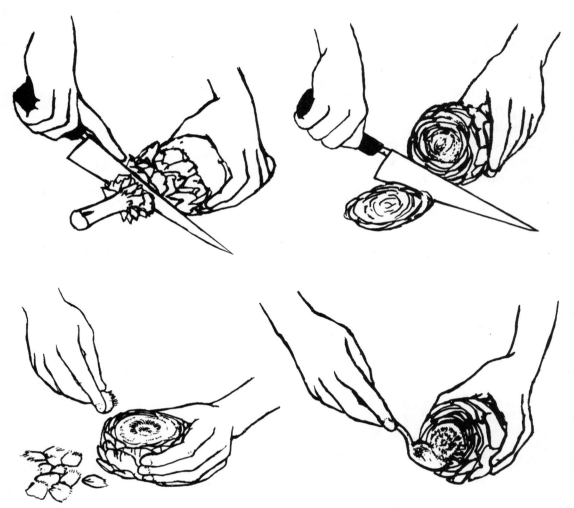

Stuffed Cabbage Rolls
Mihshi Malfoof
محشي ملفوف

Stuffing:

1 cup uncooked medium grain white rice
2 cups chopped fresh parsley leaves
½ cup chopped fresh mint leaves
4 cloves garlic, minced
1 medium white onion, finely chopped
1 bunch scallions, finely chopped
½ cup fresh lemon juice
2 teaspoons salt
½ teaspoon cinnamon
½ teaspoon allspice
½ cup olive oil

1 medium cabbage

5 cloves garlic, diced
½ cup tomato purée mixed with 1 cup water
1 teaspoon salt

½ cup fresh lemon juice
1½ teaspoons dried mint

Rinse the rice in cold water several times, and drain. Add the parsley, mint, 4 cloves minced garlic, onion, scallions, lemon juice, salt, cinnamon, and allspice to the rice. Mix while adding the olive oil.

Bring 2 quarts of water to a boil in a large, heavy saucepan. Blanch the cabbage in the boiling water, and cut off the leaves that have softened. Return the remaining cabbage to the water for 3 minutes, repeating this process until all the leaves have softened. Slice each leaf in half on the ribs, then slice part of the ribs off (see illustration). The ribs will be used later on in this recipe.

Spread the cabbage leaves on a wooden board. Fill the center of each leaf with 2 teaspoons of the filling, and spread within ½ inch from the edges of the leaf. Fold the base of the leaf over the filling, and roll as for a jelly roll. Gently squeeze each roll.

Place the cabbage ribs in the bottom of a large, heavy-bottomed pot, and place the stuffed cabbage leaves on top. Arrange the stuffed leaves side by side, and stack in layers. Sprinkle 3 cloves of the diced garlic between each layer. Add the tomato purée. Pour water over the rolls until it reaches ½ inch higher than the last layer of leaves.

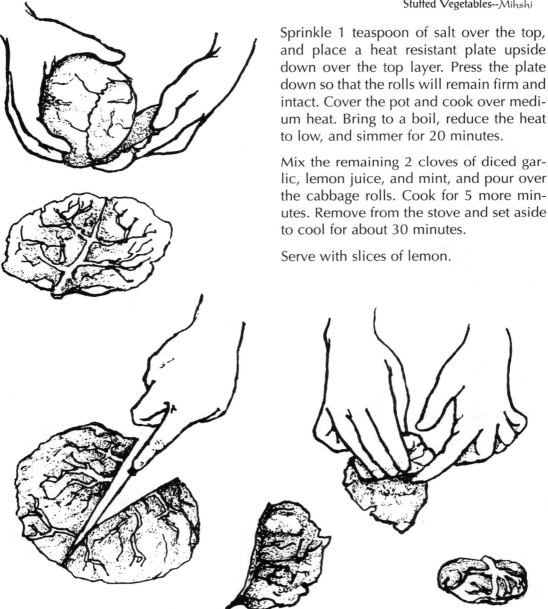

Sprinkle 1 teaspoon of salt over the top, and place a heat resistant plate upside down over the top layer. Press the plate down so that the rolls will remain firm and intact. Cover the pot and cook over medium heat. Bring to a boil, reduce the heat to low, and simmer for 20 minutes.

Mix the remaining 2 cloves of diced garlic, lemon juice, and mint, and pour over the cabbage rolls. Cook for 5 more minutes. Remove from the stove and set aside to cool for about 30 minutes.

Serve with slices of lemon.

Serves 6-8

Per serving: calories: 229, protein: 2 gm., carbohydrates: 21 gm., fat: 14 gm.

Stuffed Chard
Mihshi Waraq Silek
محشي ورق سلق

3 quarts water
2 pounds Swiss chard (save the ribs
for Swiss Chard Dip, pg. 95)

4 cups finely chopped fresh parsley
2 cups finely chopped fresh mint
4 medium ripe tomatoes, diced
2 cups uncooked medium grain rice
2 teaspoons cinnamon
2 teaspoons allspice
1 cup olive oil
2 tablespoons salt
1½ cups lemon juice

3 medium potatoes, cut into 1½-inch
pieces
lemon wedges for garnish
black and green olives for garnish

Bring the water to a boil in a large pot, and blanch the Swiss chard. Slice each leaf in half by cutting the center rib. If the rib is thick, remove it and save for later use.

Mix all the remaining ingredients, except the potatoes, ½ cup of the olive oil, 1 table-spoon of salt, and ¼ cup of the lemon juice. Place 1 tablespoon of filling on the middle of each half leaf, and spread lengthwise. Roll, folding in both ends after the first roll to secure the filling. Squeeze gently before placing in the pan. Save the excess juice.

Place the potato pieces on the bottom of a large, heavy-bottomed pot, and sprinkle with the remaining ½ cup olive oil. Arrange the stuffed Swiss chard in rows on top of the potatoes, and layer. Sprinkle with the remaining 1 tablespoon salt. Place a heat resistant plate upside down over the top layer of the stuffed Swiss chard. Gently press the plate down. Add enough water and excess juice to cover 1 inch above the plate. Cover the pot, bring to a boil, reduce the heat, and simmer for 25 minutes. Add the remaining ¼ cup of lemon juice before serving.

Arrange the stuffed Swiss chard on a large plate, and garnish with lemon wedges and black and green olives. Serve cold.

Serves 8-10

Per serving: calories: 326, protein: 4 gm., carbohydrates: 34 gm., fat: 22 gm.

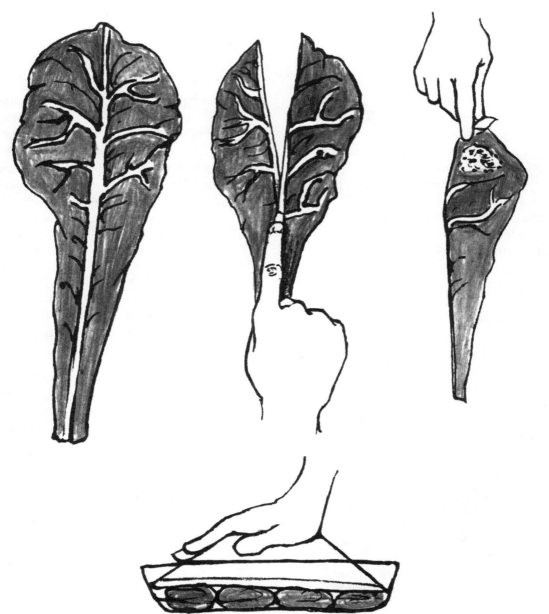

Stuffed Eggplant
Mihshi Batinjan
محشي باتنجان

2 pounds small eggplants

1 cup uncooked medium white rice
½ cup dried chick-peas, soaked
  overnight and skinned
½ bunch fresh parsley, leaves picked
  and chopped
¼ cup finely chopped fresh mint
1 medium white onion, finely chopped
¾ cup fresh lemon juice
½ cup olive oil
1 teaspoon allspice
1 tablespoon cinnamon
salt to taste

3 large ripe tomatoes, sliced
2 cloves garlic, chopped
½ teaspoon salt

1 tablespoon dried mint
1½ cups tomato sauce

Wash the eggplants and roll between the palms of your hands to soften them. This makes it easier to scoop out the insides. Slice off the stem ends, sprinkle the cut end with a little salt, and let set at room temperature for about 10 minutes. Scoop out the flesh of the eggplants with a mankara (see illustration) or melon baller, using slow strokes, until no flesh is left.

Rinse the rice in cold water several times, drain, and place in a large bowl. Add the chick-peas, parsley, mint, onion, ½ cup of the lemon juice, olive oil, seasonings (only 1 teaspoon of cinnamon), and salt. Mix well.

Stuff the eggplants with the rice mixture until half full. Arrange in a large pot, and add 1½ cups water. Add the remaining 2 teaspoons of cinnamon, the tomatoes, garlic, and ½ teaspoon salt. Cover, bring to a boil, and cook over medium heat for 45 minutes. Add the remaining ¼ cup of lemon juice, the mint, and the tomato sauce, and cook for 5 more minutes.

Serve warm.

Serves 6

Per serving: calories: 359, protein: 5 gm., carbohydrates: 39 gm., fat: 22 gm.

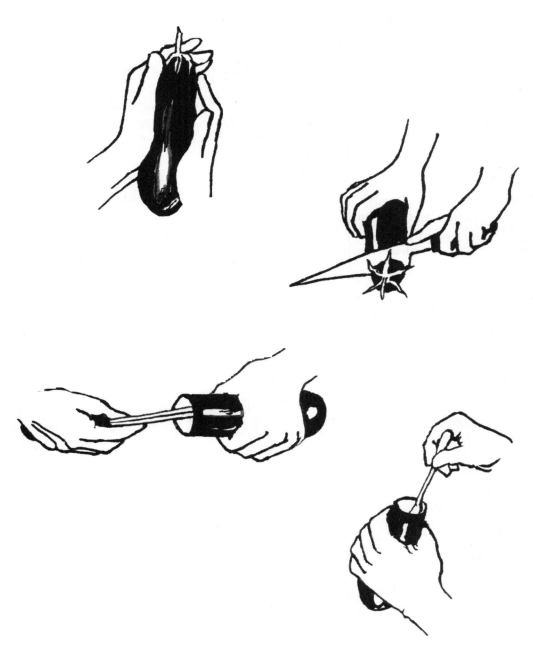

Stuffed Grape Leaves
Mihshi Waraq Bi-Inab
محشي ورق عنب

One of Lebanon's most loved dishes, warak-bi-inab is well worth the effort. Late spring or early summer is when most Lebanese prefer to make this dish, since the grape leaves are young and ten- der then. However, many people cure the leaves and use them year round to make this fabulous dish. It can be eaten as a main course or served as part of a standard mezza.

3 medium tomatoes, peeled and diced
2 bunches scallions, chopped
1 large white onion, chopped

2 cups uncooked medium white rice
1½ tablespoons salt
1 tablespoon allspice
1 tablespoon ground cinnamon
3 bunches fresh parsley, finely chopped
2 tablespoons dried mint, or 1 cup finely chopped fresh mint leaves
1½ cups extra-virgin olive oil

1 pound grape leaves, fresh or canned, soaked in water for 1 hour and drained

2 medium potatoes, sliced
2 tablespoons olive oil

2 cups water
2 teaspoons salt

1½ cups fresh lemon juice
lemon wedges for garnish

Mix the tomatoes, scallions, and onion. Add the rice, 1½ tablespoons salt, all-spice, cinnamon, parsley, mint, and olive oil to the vegetables, and mix well. Stuff the grape leaves with the vegetable and rice filling. Roll half way and fold in both ends to secure the filling (see illustration), then finish rolling.

Place a layer of sliced potatoes on the bottom of a cooking pot greased with 2 tablespoons olive oil. Arrange the rolled grape leaves in rows over the potatoes. Add the 2 cups water and 2 teaspoons salt. Cover the top layer of grape leaves with a heat-resistant plate. (This is done so the stuffed leaves don't fall apart when the water boils.) Bring to a boil, reduce the heat to low, and cook for 40 minutes. Add the lemon juice and serve hot or cold. Garnish with fresh lemon wedges.

Serves 8-10

Per serving: calories: 456, protein: 3 gm., carbohydrates: 30 gm., fat: 34 gm.

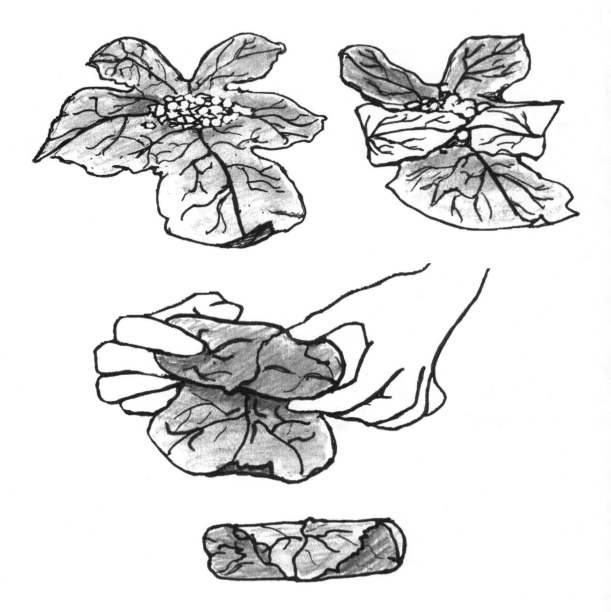

Stuffed Green Peppers
Flayfleh Mehshiye
فليفة محشية

4 large green peppers

1 cup uncooked white rice
1 large ripe tomato, diced
1 small white onion, finely chopped
¼ cup fresh lemon juice
3 cloves garlic, minced
¼ teaspoon cinnamon
¼ teaspoon allspice
1 teaspoon salt
⅓ cup olive oil

1 cup tomato sauce mixed with ½ cup water

Hollow out the green peppers, carefully remove all the seeds, and rinse several times in cold water. Drain.

Mix the rice, tomato, onion, lemon juice, garlic, and seasonings. Add the olive oil and mix again. Divide the rice mixture among the green peppers, and fill.

Grease the bottom of a small cooking pot with olive oil. Line up the stuffed peppers inside the pot. Cover with the water and tomato sauce, cover the pot, and cook for 35 minutes over medium-low heat, or until the rice is tender. You can add more water if necessary to keep some liquid in the pot.

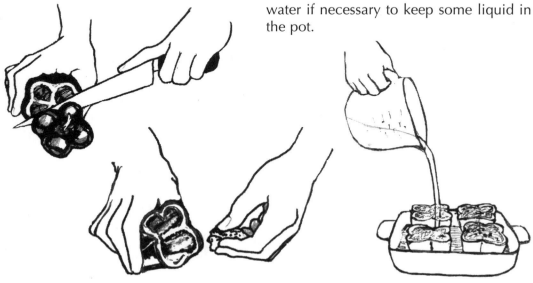

Serves 4

Per serving: calories: 300, protein: 3 gm., carbohydrates: 29 gm., fat: 20 gm.

Swiss Chard Dip
Mtabbal Silek
سلق

This dip is served on the side of Stuffed Chard (Mihishi Waraq Silek), page 88.

Tahini Sauce:
3 medium cloves garlic, minced
2½ teaspoons salt
1 cup tahini
1 cup water
1 cup fresh lemon juice

2 bunches Swiss chard (or the unused ribs from Stuffed Chard, pg. 88)
4 cups water

¼ cup fresh lemon juice
½ teaspoon salt

2 tablespoons olive oil

To prepare the tahini sauce, mix the garlic with the salt, and add the tahini. Add the water, mixing gradually. Beat the mixture for 1 minute with a fork. Gradually add the lemon juice, and blend well. Set aside.

Cut the ribs off the chard leaves. The leaves can be used to prepare Stuffed Chard (Mihshi Waraq Silek) on page 88. Remove the strings from the ribs. Rinse the ribs in cold water several times, and drain. Cut the ribs into 2-inch pieces.

Place the 4 cups water in a saucepan, and bring to a boil. Add the ribs and cook for 15-20 minutes or until the ribs are tender. Drain, place in a food processor, and finely chop. Transfer to a large bowl, and add the tahini sauce, lemon juice, and salt. Mix well.

Spread on a large platter, and sprinkle the olive oil on top of the dip. Serve cold with pita bread.

Serves 4-6
Per serving: calories: 393, protein: 10 gm., carbohydrates: 21 gm., fat: 30 gm.

Stuffed Zucchini
Mihshi Koosa
محشي كوسى

To scoop out the inside of the zucchini, you can use a special tool, similar to an apple corer, called a "mankara." It is available at any Middle Eastern or Lebanese food store.

1 cup uncooked medium grain rice

½ bunch fresh parsley, leaves picked and chopped
½ bunch fresh mint, leaves picked and chopped
2 large ripe tomatoes, diced
1 small white onion, finely chopped
1 tablespoon salt
1 teaspoon allspice
1 teaspoon cinnamon
¼ cup olive oil

2 pounds small green zucchini (8 small)

6 cloves garlic, minced
¼ cup fresh lemon juice
1 tablespoon tomato paste mixed with 1 cup water

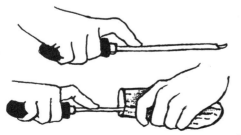

Rinse the rice in cold water several times, and drain. Place in a large bowl. Add the parsley, mint, tomatoes, and onion. Mix well with 2 teaspoons of the salt, the allspice, cinnamon, and olive oil.

Wash the zucchini and slice off the stem end. Dip the open end of the zucchini in salt. Scoop out its flesh with the mankara (see illustration) or a melon baller, scraping the insides with slow strokes until no flesh remains. Be careful not to puncture the zucchini or your hand! Save the flesh for the Zucchini Stew (Al-Mnazalet Koosa) or Zucchini Omelet (Ojhet Al-Koosa) (pages 138 and 139).

Wash the hollowed-out zucchini, and stuff them with the rice stuffing. Fill only half way, so that they don't burst open when the rice swells up while cooking.

Arrange the stuffed zucchini in a large, heavy-bottomed pot, and add the tomato paste mixture. Add enough water to cover them. Add 1 or 2 more teaspoons of salt. Cover and cook over medium heat for 40 minutes. Mix the garlic and lemon juice, and add to the zucchini. Cook for 5 more

Serves 6

Per serving: calories: 178, protein: 3 gm., carbohydrates: 21 gm., fat: 9 gm.

Legumes

Fasoolia Wadas

فاصولية وعدس

Beans and Eggs
Fool Maa Beyd
فول مع بيض

1 small white onion, chopped
¼ cup olive oil
4 cups fresh green fava beans
½ cup water

½ teaspoon ground cumin
1 teaspoon salt
¼ teaspoon black pepper
dash cinnamon
4 eggs

Sauté the onion in the olive oil until limp. Add the beans and stir well. Sauté on medium heat for about 5 minutes. Add ½ cup water, cover, and simmer over low heat for about 20 minutes until the beans are tender but not mushy.

Add the seasonings and eggs. Stir gently and cook until the eggs are set. Serve with pita bread and Yogurt Sauce (Salaset Al-Laban), page 34.

Serves 4

Per serving: calories: 400, protein: 18 gm., carbohydrates: 36 gm., fat: 22 gm.

Breakfast Fava Beans
Fool
فول

2 (15-ounce) cans fava beans

¼ cup extra-virgin olive oil
juice of 2 lemons
1 clove garlic, minced
salt to taste
½ cup finely chopped fresh parsley

1 large tomato, sliced
1 cucumber, sliced
1 bunch fresh radishes
10 black olives
fresh mint leaves

Rinse and drain the canned fava beans, and place in a medium pot with enough water to cover. Heat until warm.

Meanwhile, mix the olive oil with the lemon juice, garlic, and salt. Drain the beans and place in a bowl. Pour the olive oil mixture and parsley over the fava beans, and combine well.

Arrange the tomato, cucumber, radishes, black olives, and mint in a separate shallow plate. Serve right away alongside the fava beans.

Serves 4
Per serving: calories: 434, protein: 16 gm., carbohydrates: 58 gm., fat: 15 gm.

Cooked Lima Beans
Fasoolia Mtaballeh
فاصولية متبلة

2 cups dried lima beans, soaked for 24 hours
½ teaspoon baking soda

2 cups chopped onions
3 cloves garlic, minced
1 cup fresh lemon juice
¼ cup extra-virgin olive oil
½ teaspoon salt
¼ cup chopped fresh parsley

Cook the beans with the baking soda and enough water to cover (about 6 cups) until tender, about 40 minutes. Rinse the beans, then drain.

Mix with the onions, garlic, lemon juice, olive oil, and salt. Garnish with the parsley and serve with warm pita bread.

Serves 4

Per serving: calories: 463, protein: 17 gm., carbohydrates: 65 gm., fat: 18 gm.

Falafel
Falafel
فلافل

Falafel is one of the oldest Middle Eastern dishes. It is made in several different countries and in many different ways, even within the same country. We have included our authentic recipe which our mother prepares from scratch.

1 cup dried fava beans, soaked overnight and drained, with skins removed
1 cup dried chick-peas, soaked overnight and drained
½ cup medium bulgur, soaked in 1 cup hot water for ½ hour and drained
3 medium white onions, chopped

3 large cloves garlic, crushed
1 teaspoon ground cumin
1 teaspoon ground coriander
¼ teaspoon chili powder
1¼ teaspoons black pepper
1 teaspoon baking soda
2½ teaspoons salt

3 cups canola oil

Mix the fava beans, chick-peas, bulgur, and onions. Put in a food processor or meat grinder, and finely grind.

Add the remaining ingredients, except for the canola oil, and mix well. Place 2 tablespoons of this falafel mixture in the palm of your hand, and press into a small patty. Alternatively, you can use a falafel spoon to make the patties. (It is available at most Middle Eastern groceries stores and is very simple to use.)

Heat the canola oil in a deep frying pan over medium heat. Drop several patties into the hot oil at a time. Fry the falafel patties until they are golden brown. Make sure to flip them once to insure that both sides are cooked equally. Remove and place on a paper towel to absorb some of the oil.

Serve warm with a plate of your favorite freshly cut vegetables.

Variation: You can add ½ cup each chopped fresh cilantro and parsley before grinding the bean mixture.

Serves 4-6

Per serving: calories: 428, protein: 11 gm., carbohydrates: 44 gm., fat: 22 gm.

Fava Beans
Fool Mudamas
فول مدمس

An excellent dish for bean lovers, this recipe is similar to the breakfast fava beans. Dried beans are used instead.

1 pound dried fava beans
1 teaspoon baking soda

4 cloves garlic, minced
¼ cup fresh lemon juice
¼ cup extra-virgin olive oil
salt to taste
¼ teaspoon cayenne (red pepper)
½ cup coarsely chopped fresh parsley

Cover the dried beans with water and 1 teaspoon of baking soda, and soak over night. Rinse several times. Cover with clean, fresh water (about 12 cups), and cook over medium heat for several hours until soft and succulent. Drain.

Mix the garlic with the lemon juice, then add the olive oil, salt, and cayenne. Mix again.

Add the mixture to the drained beans, and garnish with the parsley. Serve warm with pita bread.

Serves 4

Per serving: calories: 263, protein: 8 gm., carbohydrates: 25 gm., fat: 17 gm.

Fava Beans with Coriander
Fool Akhdar Bi-Kizbara
فول أخضر بكزبرة

4 cups green fava beans

1 medium white onion, chopped
½ cup olive oil
6 large cloves garlic, minced
1 bunch cilantro, coarsely chopped

1½ cups water
1½ teaspoons salt

¼ cup fresh lemon juice

Remove the strings and trim the ends from the fava beans, and cut into 3-inch pieces. Wash in cold water and drain.

Sauté the onion in the olive oil until golden brown. Add the garlic and cilantro, stir, and cook over medium heat for 5 more minutes. Add the fava beans, sauté for a few minutes, and cover the pot.

Lower the heat and cook for 10 more minutes. Uncover, add the water and salt, and simmer for 10 more minutes. Add the lemon juice and serve hot or cold with pita bread.

Serves 6
Per serving: calories: 296, protein: 8 gm., carbohydrates: 26 gm., fat: 17 gm.

Lentil Stew
Moujadara Majrouche
مجدرة مجروشة

This delicious stew may be eaten hot or cold. It is best served with a tomato salad and warm pita bread. Yellow lentils are available at Middle Eastern stores.

1½ cups dried yellow lentils
6 cups water

2 medium white onions, finely chopped
½ cup olive oil
½ cup uncooked white rice
2 teaspoons salt
1 teaspoon ground cumin

Rinse the lentils and place in a 3-quart pot. Add the water and cook on medium heat for 30 minutes.

Sauté the onions in the olive oil. Add the rice, onions, salt, and cumin to the lentils. Cover, and simmer for 25 minutes, or until the rice is done. Stir and serve.

Serves 6

Per serving: calories: 322, protein: 9 gm., carbohydrates: 31 gm., fat: 17 gm.

Lentils and Rice
Moujadara
مجدرة

This is a delicious and nutritious dish that is best served with Cucumber and Tomato Salad (Salatet Khiar Bi-Banadoora), page 58.

1 cup uncooked lentils

1 cup uncooked long grain rice
2 teaspoons salt

2 large red onions, julienned
¼ cup extra-virgin olive oil
3 cups water

Rinse the lentils in cold water, drain, and place in a cooking pot. Add 3 cups of water, bring to a boil, then cook over medium heat for 15 minutes.

Add the rice and salt, return to a boil, lower the heat, and simmer on low another 15 minutes, or until the rice and lentils are tender.

Sauté the onions in the olive oil until golden brown. Add to the cooked rice and lentils, and gently mix. Serve right away.

Serves 4
Per serving: calories: 495, protein: 11 gm., carbohydrates: 51 gm., fat 27 gm.

Lentils in Lemon Juice
Adas Bi-Hamod
عدس بحامض

Lentils are an excellent source of protein.

4 cloves garlic, crushed
juice of 3 large lemons
½ teaspoon salt
2 cups cooked lentils
⅓ cup extra-virgin olive oil
½ bunch fresh parsley, chopped

Mix the garlic, lemon juice, and salt. Pour over the lentils, and mix well. Add the extra-virgin olive oil, and garnish with the parsley.

Serve hot or cold with pita bread and a plate of your favorite vegetables, olives, and pickles.

Serves 4

Per serving: calories: 293, protein: 8 gm., carbohydrates: 23 gm., fat: 20 gm.

Lentils with Bulgur
Moujadara Bi-Burghul
مجدرة ببرغل

This main dish is best served with Tomato Salad (Salatet Al-Banadoora), page 67.

1 cup dried lentils
6 cups water

1 large white onion, finely chopped
¼ cup extra-virgin olive oil
½ cup medium bulgur

Rinse the lentils and place in a cooking pot. Cover with the water, and bring to a boil. Reduce the heat to medium, and cook for 20 minutes.

Sauté the onion in the olive oil until golden brown. Add the onion to the lentils, and cook for 5 more minutes.

Add the bulgur, cover, and simmer until the bulgur is tender and the water is absorbed.

Serve hot or cold with plain yogurt or tomato salad.

Serves 6
Per serving: calories: 211, protein: 7 gm., carbohydrates: 25 gm., fat: 9 gm.

From the Tables of Lebanon

Rice and Pasta
Riz/Macaroni
معكرونة/رز

Green Fava Beans with Rice
Fool Bi-Riz
فول برز

3 cups fresh green fava beans (about 2 pounds in the pods)

1 cup chopped onions
½ cup olive oil

1 cup medium white grain rice
1½ teaspoons salt
½ teaspoon cinnamon
½ teaspoon allspice
2 cups water

½ cup pistachios

Remove the fava beans from the pods, wash several times in cold water, and drain.

Sauté the onions in the olive oil until golden. Add the fava beans and sauté for 5 more minutes. Add the rice and seasonings, and stir once. Add the water and bring to a boil. Lower the heat, cover, and simmer until the rice is done, about 15 minutes.

Uncover the pot and stir gently. Garnish with the pistachios and serve hot with a side dish of plain yogurt.

Serves 6

Per serving: calories: 338, protein: 14 gm., carbohydrates: 53 gm., fat: 7 gm.

Lebanese Rice
Riz Bi-Sheereeyee
رز بشعرية

Sautéing the vermicelli produces an unforgettable fragrance, a common and pleasant aroma enjoyed daily in many Lebanese kitchens.

3 tablespoons olive oil or canola oil
⅓ cup vermicelli, broken into ½-inch pieces

1 cup uncooked long grain white rice

2 cups water
1½ teaspoons salt

Heat the oil in a small pot, and brown the vermicelli (do not burn it!). Wash the rice in cold water, and rinse. Add to the vermicelli and stir for 1 minute.

Add the water and salt, and bring to a boil. Lower the heat, cover, and simmer for about 15 minutes. Do not stir. The rice is done when all the water is absorbed and the vermicelli is flaky (usually about 15 minutes).

Serve with plain nonfat yogurt.

Serves 4
Per serving: calories: 255, protein: 4 gm., carbohydrates: 36 gm., fat: 9 gm.

Rice in Tomato Sauce
Riz Bi-Salset Al-Banadoora
رز بصلطة البندورة

1 small white onion, finely chopped
¼ cup olive oil

3 large ripe tomatoes, peeled, seeded, and diced
1½ cups water
1 teaspoon salt
½ teaspoon allspice
½ teaspoon cinnamon
dash of black pepper

1 cup uncooked long grain white rice, washed and drained

Sauté the onion in the olive oil until slightly golden. Add the tomatoes, water, and spices, and bring to a gentle boil. Add the rice, stir once, and bring to a boil again.

Reduce the heat, cover, and simmer for 25 minutes, or until all the water has evaporated. When the rice is done, turn off the heat and stir the rice with a fork. Cover and let set for 5 more minutes.

Serve warm.

Serves 4

Per serving: calories: 275, protein: 3 gm., carbohydrates: 32 gm., fat: 17 gm.

Rice with Zucchini
Koosa Bi-Riz
كوسى برز

4 quarts water
4 large zucchini or yellow crook neck
  squash, cubed (1½ pounds)

2 cups coarsely chopped onions
⅓ cup olive oil

4 large cloves garlic, minced

1 cup uncooked long grain white rice
1 teaspoon salt
¼ teaspoon allspice
½ teaspoon cinnamon

Bring the water to a boil in a medium cooking pot. Add the zucchini and cook for 5 minutes. Remove the zucchini from the water, and reserve 2 cups of the cooking water for later use.

Sauté the onions in the olive oil in a large sauté pan over medium heat for 3 minutes. Add the garlic, stir for 2 more minutes, and add the zucchini.

Stir in the rice, seasonings, and 2 cups reserved water. Bring to a boil. Cover and simmer for 20 more minutes, or until all the water is evaporated.

Serve hot with a side dish of plain nonfat yogurt.

Serves 6
Per serving: calories: 197, protein: 2 gm., carbohydrates: 21 gm., fat: 10 gm.

Spinach with Rice
Sbanegh Bi-Riz
سبانغ برز

1 large onion, chopped
½ cup olive oil
2 bunches fresh spinach, well washed
  and finely chopped

2 cups water
1 teaspoon allspice
1 teaspoon cinnamon
2 teaspoons salt

3 cups Cooked Rice, pg. 30
1 lemon, cut in wedges for garnish

Sauté the onion in the olive oil until golden brown, add the spinach, and cook until the spinach is limp.

Add the water and seasonings, and simmer over medium-low heat for 20 minutes.

Meanwhile, prepare the Cooked Rice (Riz Mfalfal). Serve the spinach to the side of the rice and lemon wedges.

Serves 4
Per serving: calories: 440, protein: 5 gm., carbohydrates: 32 gm., fat: 31 gm.

Spaghetti in Garlic Sauce
Macaroni Bi-Toom
معكرونة بثوم

For the garlic lovers! This is a side dish that can easily be doubled to serve as an entree.

¼ cup olive oil
6 large cloves garlic, minced
1 cup nonfat plain yogurt
3 tablespoons finely chopped fresh
 parsley
1 teaspoon salt
½ teaspoon pepper

2 cups cooked spaghetti

Heat the olive oil in a heavy saucepan. Sauté the garlic until slightly golden. Add the yogurt, 2 tablespoons of the parsley, and the salt and pepper. Stir well and cook over low heat for 5 minutes.

Pour the hot sauce over the warm spaghetti, and mix well. Garnish with the remaining parsley, and serve right away.

Serves 4

Per serving: calories: 255, protein: 7 gm., carbohydrates: 26 gm., fat: 13 gm.

Spaghetti in Tomato Sauce
Macaroni Bi-Banadoora
معكرونة ببندورة

This is a side dish that can easily be doubled to serve as an entree.

3 tablespoons olive oil
2 large cloves garlic, minced

6 medium ripe tomatoes, peeled, seeded, and diced
1 teaspoon finely chopped fresh parsley
½ teaspoon salt
½ teaspoon black pepper

1½ cups cooked spaghetti

Heat the olive oil in a saucepan, and sauté the garlic until lightly golden brown.

Add the tomatoes, parsley, salt, and pepper. Lower the heat and simmer for 15-20 minutes.

Pour over the hot spaghetti, and mix well. Serve hot.

Serves 3

Per serving: calories: 265, protein: 5 gm., carbohydrates: 30 gm., fat 14 gm.

Spaghetti in Yogurt Sauce
Macaroni Bi-Laban
معكرونة بلبن

When preparing this book, our friends loved tasting this recipe. It is easy to make and delicious. Use as a side dish, or double the amounts for an entree.

2 medium cloves garlic, minced
2 cups nonfat plain yogurt
1 teaspoon salt
2 teaspoons dried mint

1½ cups cooked spaghetti

Mix the garlic, yogurt, and salt in a small bowl. Sprinkle in the mint and mix well.

Add the dressing to the warm spaghetti, and serve right away.

Serves 3
Per serving: calories: 191, protein: 14 gm., carbohydrates: 33 gm., fat: 0 gm.

Spaghetti with Eggplant
Macaroni Bi-Batinjan
معكرونة بباتنجان

This can serve up to 12 as a side dish.

1 pound long eggplants, peeled
1 cup olive oil

1½ pounds ripe tomatoes, peeled and
    seeded
1 large white onion, finely chopped
2 fresh green peppers, thinly sliced
3 cloves garlic, minced
1 teaspoon salt
½ teaspoon allspice
½ teaspoon crushed thyme leaves
dash nutmeg
1 cup hot water

1 cup shredded mozzarella
1 cup shredded provolone or Gruyère
1 pound uncooked spaghetti

Slice the eggplants ½ inch thick. Fry in the olive oil until golden. Place on a paper towel to drain.

To make the tomato sauce, cut the tomatoes into small pieces, and fry in the remaining oil. Add the onions and fry for 2 more minutes. Add the green pepper, and mix well. Add the garlic and stir with the seasonings. Add the hot water, cover, and simmer for 10 more minutes.

Cook the spaghetti as directed on the package. Preheat the oven to 350°F. Then place half the spaghetti in a baking dish, and cover with half the eggplants, half the tomato sauce, and half of the cheese. Repeat with the remainder of the spaghetti, eggplants, tomato sauce, and cheese. Cover with aluminum foil, and bake for 15 minutes.

Serves 6

118
Per serving: calories: 609, protein: 15 gm., carbohydrates: 36 gm., fat: 44 gm.

Vegetarian Lasagne
Lazagna Bi-Alkhodar
لازنية بخضار

1 pound frozen broccoli, or 4 large
fresh zucchini, thinly sliced

1 cup finely chopped onions
3 cloves garlic, minced
½ cup olive oil
2 teaspoons crushed basil
2 teaspoons oregano
1 bay leaf
1 teaspoon salt
1 teaspoon black pepper
12 ounces tomato paste
1 pound canned whole tomatoes
1 cup water

6 cooked lasagne noodles
3 cups shredded mozzarella
1 cup grated Parmesan

Place the broccoli or zucchini in a steamer, and steam until half done.

In a sauté pan, sauté the onions and garlic in ¼ cup of the olive oil until limp. Add 1 teaspoon of the basil, 1 teaspoon of the oregano, the bay leaf, salt, black pepper, tomato paste, and whole tomatoes. Add the water and cook over medium-low heat for 30 minutes. Adjust the seasonings as desired.

Meanwhile, sauté the steamed broccoli or zucchini in the remaining ¼ cup olive oil until limp.

Preheat the oven to 350°F. Place 1 cup of the tomato sauce in the bottom of a rectangular baking pan, and add half of the noodles. Add the broccoli and half the remaining sauce with half of the mozzarella and Parmesan cheese. Top with the remaining noodles and sauce. Sprinkle on 1 teaspoon of the oregano, 1 teaspoon of the basil, and the remaining cheese.

Cover the pan with aluminum foil, and bake for 45 minutes. Then remove the foil and bake for 15 more minutes.

Serve hot.

Serves 6-8

Per serving: calories: 497, protein: 22 gm., carbohydrates: 35 gm., fat: 29 gm.

From the Tables of Lebanon

Entrees

Mookadamat

مقدامات

Artichoke Stew
Ardichaouki Bi-Khodar
ارضي شوكة بخضار

12 small artichoke hearts

2 large carrots, sliced

12 pearl onions
½ cup olive oil
1 cup green peas
2 medium red potatoes, cut into
  2-inch pieces

2 tablespoons flour
3 cups water
1 teaspoon salt
1 teaspoon white pepper

Bring some water to boil in a large saucepan. Add the artichoke hearts and ½ teaspoon salt, and cook for 5 minutes. Remove and drain.

Add the carrots and cook for 5 more minutes. Remove the carrots and save the water.

Add the onions to the saucepan, and sauté in the olive oil until golden. Add the artichoke hearts, carrots, peas, and potatoes, and sauté for 5 more minutes.

Dissolve the flour in ½ cup of the cooking water, and add to the artichoke hearts. Stir all the vegetables into the flour and water mixture. Add the salt and pepper, to taste. Cover the pot and cook until all the vegetables are tender.

Serve warm or cold on a plate garnished with lemon wedges.

Serves 5
Per serving: calories: 347, protein: 5 gm., carbohydrates: 34 gm., fat: 21 gm.

Bulgur with Tomatoes
Burghul Bi-Banadoora

Quick, easy, and simply delicious.

2 large white onions, finely chopped
½ cup olive oil

4 cups ripe whole tomatoes
2 cups tomato juice
1 tablespoon salt

2½ cups medium bulgur

Sauté the onions in the olive oil until golden. Add the tomatoes, tomato juice, and salt, and cook on medium heat for 20 minutes.

Add the bulgur, cover, and simmer on low heat for 30 minutes. Stir gently and serve right away.

Serves 6
Per serving: calories: 438, protein: 10 gm., carbohydrates: 58 gm., fat: 17 gm.

Chick-Peas with Arabic Bread Croutons
Fattet Al-Hummus
فتة الحمص

Fattet al-humus is dish served mostly to friends and visitors for brunch on relaxed weekends or weekdays.

2 tablespoons olive oil or canola oil
2 Arabic breads, cut in small pieces

4 cups cooked chick-peas, with 1 cup of their cooking liquid
1 tablespoon salt
2 tablespoons cumin

2 tablespoons dried mint
3 cups nonfat plain yogurt
3 cloves garlic, crushed

⅓ cup warm extra-virgin olive oil

Heat the 2 tablespoons of olive oil in a sauté pan, and brown the pita bread.

In a large bowl, mix the hot, cooked chick-peas with the cooking liquid, salt, and 1 tablespoon of the cumin.

In a separate bowl, mix the dried mint, yogurt, and garlic. Add to the chick-peas, and top with the ⅓ cup warmed olive oil. Add the remaining 1 tablespoon of cumin, and season with salt to taste.

Serve hot.

Serves 6

Per serving: calories: 450, protein: 18 gm., carbohydrates: 49 gm., fat: 19 gm.

Eggplant and Chick-Pea Casserole
Msakaa

Msakaa is a very popular summer dish in the southern part of Lebanon. Msakaa means cold, making it an appropriate dish to serve in the summer!

2 large eggplants, peeled and sliced into 4-inch pieces

2 cups chopped white onions
½ cup olive oil
2 cups cooked chick-peas

6 large cloves garlic, minced
½ cup tomato purée
1 cup water

3½ teaspoons salt
½ teaspoon allspice
½ teaspoon cinnamon

4 ripe tomatoes

2 teaspoons dried mint

Soak the sliced eggplant in enough water to cover with 2 teaspoons of salt for 15-20 minutes. This decreases how much olive oil they will absorb.

Sauté the onions in the olive oil until lightly brown. Add the chick-peas and stir for 2 minutes. Remove, carefully draining the excess oil, and set aside. In the same olive oil, fry the eggplant until golden brown. Remove and place on a paper towel to absorb the excess oil.

Sauté the garlic in the same pan over medium heat for 3-5 minutes. Remove and add to the onions. Dissolve the tomato purée in 1 cup water. Pour over the chick-peas, onions, and garlic. Add the seasonings. Transfer the chick-pea mixture back to the pan, and simmer for 5 minutes.

Preheat the oven to 350°F. Place the fried eggplant in a casserole dish. Pour the chick-pea mixture on top. Slice the tomatoes into wedges, and arrange them on top of the chick-peas. Sprinkle on the mint and bake for 20 minutes.

You can serve hot or cold.

Serves 8-10

Per serving: calories: 455, protein: 5 gm., carbohydrates: 28 gm., fat: 28 gm.

Eggplant and Garbanzo Stew
Mnazalet Al-Batinjan
منذلة الباتنجان

Eggplants are very common throughout the Mediterranean, so they are included in many dishes. Try this delicious recipe!

1 medium onion, coarsely chopped
¾ cup olive oil
2 cups cooked or canned chick-peas
4 fresh ripe tomatoes, peeled and cut in wedges

2 large eggplants, peeled and sliced 3 inches thick

3 tablespoons dried mint
salt to taste

Sauté the onion in the olive oil until golden. Remove the onion to a large saucepan. Add the chick-peas and tomatoes, and cook for 15 minutes.

Fry the eggplant in the hot oil until golden brown. Add to the chick-peas and cook until the eggplant is soft.

Add the mint and season with salt to taste.

Serves 6

Per serving: calories: 416, protein: 6 gm., carbohydrates: 31 gm., fat: 33 gm.

Eggplant with Yogurt Sauce
Batinjan Bi-Laban
باتنجان بلبن

2 eggplants, peeled and cut into 1-inch cubes
1 cup canola oil

Yogurt Sauce:
1 cup plain yogurt
5 cloves garlic, minced
½ teaspoon crushed dried mint leaves
salt to taste

Soak the eggplants in salted water (½ teaspoon of salt per cup of water) for 1 hour. Rinse and drain well.

Heat the canola oil in a frying pan, and add the eggplant. Fry until golden brown. Remove and arrange on a paper towel to absorb the excess oil.

Meanwhile, make a yogurt sauce by mixing the yogurt, garlic, mint, and a dash of salt to taste.

Arrange the warm eggplant on a shallow plate, and pour over the yogurt sauce. Serve right away.

Serves 5
Per serving: calories: 248, protein: 3 gm., carbohydrates: 16 gm., fat: 22 gm.

Eggplant Stew
Msabahet Al-Batinjan
مسبحة الباتنجان

4 large tomatoes

⅓ cup olive oil
1 large onion, coarsely chopped
3 cloves garlic, minced

1 teaspoon salt
½ teaspoon black pepper
¼ teaspoon ground cumin (optional)

¾ cup water
4 zucchini, peeled and cut into 1-inch cubes
2 eggplants, peeled and cut into 1-inch cubes

To peel the tomatoes, dip them into boiling water for 20 seconds, then plunge into ice water. The skins should slip off. Cut the tomatoes into large wedges, and remove the seeds.

Pour the olive oil into a large sauté pan, and sauté the onion and garlic until golden. Add the salt, pepper, cumin, and tomatoes. Cover and cook over medium heat for 7 minutes. Add the water, zucchini, and eggplant, and bring to a boil. Lower the heat and cook for 35 minutes.

You may serve this cold or warm. You can adjust amount of salt, black pepper, and cumin to taste.

Serves 5

Per serving: calories: 247, protein: 3 gm., carbohydrates: 33 gm., fat: 18 gm.

Eggs with Sumac
Beyd Bi-Summac
بيض بسماق

Sumac has a tart taste similar in flavor to lemon.

2 red potatoes, cubed
½ cup olive oil

4 eggs

1 tablespoon sumac powder
½ cup water
1 tablespoon red vinegar
1 teaspoon dried mint
½ teaspoon salt
2 cloves garlic, minced
½ teaspoon white pepper

Fry the potatoes in the olive oil. Remove the potatoes and drain. Fry the eggs in remaining oil for about 5 minutes over medium heat. Drain off the extra oil, leaving the eggs in the pan.

Meanwhile, mix the sumac powder with the water, vinegar, mint, salt, garlic, and pepper. Add this mixture to the eggs, and fry for 2 more minutes. Add the potatoes and mix well.

Serve hot with pita bread.

Serves 4
Per serving: calories: 149, protein: 7 gm., carbohydrates: 15 gm., fat: 9 gm.

Fried Cabbage with Bulgur
Makmura
مكمورة

1 cup medium bulgur

1 small head cabbage

⅓ cup olive oil
1 large onion, thinly sliced

½ teaspoon salt
½ teaspoon black pepper

Place the bulgur in a bowl, cover with boiling water, and stir. Soak for 30 minutes and drain any excess water.

Meanwhile, wash the cabbage and shred in a food processor.

Heat the olive oil in a large pan, and fry the onion until golden brown. Add the cabbage, cover, and fry over medium-low heat for about 15 minutes, stirring frequently. Uncover the pan and cook for 10 more minutes.

Add the bulgur and stir. Add the salt and pepper, cover again, and cook for 15 more minutes. Stir once.

Serve warm.

Serves 4-6

Per serving: calories: 340, protein: 7 gm., carbohydrates: 44 gm., fat: 16 gm.

Okra with Tomatoes and Olive Oil
Bemya Bi-Zeyt
بمية بزيت

You will love this recipe, even if you're not an okra lover!

1½ pounds fresh okra
½ cup olive oil or canola oil

1 cup diced onions

1 cup chopped fresh cilantro
5 large cloves garlic, minced

1 cup water
5 medium tomatoes, peeled and diced
½ cup tomato purée

1½ teaspoons salt
¼ teaspoon black pepper

¼ cup fresh lemon juice

Cut off the stem ends of the okra pods. Wash in cold water and drain. Heat the olive oil in a sauté pan, and fry the okra. Remove and set aside.

Add the onions to the pan, and sauté until slightly brown. Add the cilantro and garlic, and stir well until limp.

Then add the water, tomatoes, and tomato purée, and bring to a boil. Add the okra, season with salt and pepper, cover, and cook on medium heat for 30 minutes.

Add the lemon juice before serving. Serve with warm pita bread.

Serves 4
Per serving: calories: 369, protein: 4 gm., carbohydrates: 27 gm., fat: 26 gm.

Omelet with Parsley
Ojhet Baadoonis
عجة بقدونس

This recipe is every Lebanese child's favorite. And Dalal's American husband, Leon, is no exception! After cooking, briefly place the omelets on paper towels to absorb some of the oil.

1 medium brown onion, finely chopped
1½ teaspoons salt
1 teaspoon allspice
1 bunch fresh parsley, finely chopped

6 medium eggs

1 teaspoon cinnamon
¼ cup sifted flour
½ teaspoon baking soda

1½ cups canola oil

romaine lettuce and tomatoes for garnish

Rub the chopped onion with 1 teaspoon of the salt and the allspice, and mix with the parsley. Beat the eggs with a fork, and add to the parsley mixture. Season with the cinnamon and the remaining salt. Gently fold in the flour and baking soda. Refrigerate the mixture for ½ hour.

After ½ hour, heat the canola oil in a large frying pan. When it is sizzling, use an ice cream scoop or a ladle to pour ¼ cup of the flour batter into the oil at a time. Spread the mixture evenly in the oil, and deep-fry both sides of the omelet, until golden brown. Repeat with more batter until all of it is used.

Serve ojeht baadoonis warm or cold on a bed of romaine lettuce and tomatoes. Alternatively, you can use them as a filling for pita bread and eat it like a sandwich.

Serves 4-6

Per serving: calories: 319, protein: 9 gm., carbohydrates: 7 gm., fat: 28 gm.

Potatoes with Eggs
Batata Bi-Beyd
بطاطا ببيض

This dish is best served hot, as soon as it is made.

4 large potatoes, peeled and cut into 1-inch cubes
1 cup canola oil

2 large eggs

½ teaspoon allspice
½ teaspoon cinnamon
1 teaspoon salt

Fry the potatoes in the canola oil until golden brown. Remove and set aside to drain on paper towels.

In a separate pan, scramble the eggs with 1 tablespoon of the canola oil. Once the eggs are done, add the potatoes and cook for 4 more minutes. Add the seasonings and salt as you mix the potatoes with the scrambled eggs.

Serve with warm pita bread and Tomato Salad (page 67).

Serves 4

Per serving: calories: 425, protein: 5 gm., carbohydrates: 34 gm., fat: 28 gm.

Spinach Pies
Fatayir Bi-Sbanegh
فطاير بسبانغ

Ever since I was little, my sister Dalal has baked these delicious spinach pies for me and the rest of the family. I remember running around the kitchen, smelling their magic aromas and waiting for them to come hot out of the oven. A sprinkle of fresh lemon juice adds a lot to their taste. Also, the vitamin C in the lemon improves the absorption of the iron in the spinach!

Sumac adds flavor to this recipe and has several health benefits (see page 18).

18 cups fresh spinach leaves, well washed and finely chopped
2 large white onions, minced and mixed with 1 tablespoon salt

2 cups fresh lemon juice
2 tablespoons sumac (optional)
1 teaspoon allspice
1 teaspoon black pepper

1½ cups olive oil

3 loaves frozen white bread dough, defrosted and risen until doubled

Place the spinach in a large salad bowl. Add the onions and salt, and mix well. Squeeze the spinach mixture, working with your fingers. Discard any liquid. Add the lemon juice, sumac, allspice, and pepper, and mix. Add the olive oil and stir well.

Preheat the oven to 450°F. Divide each loaf of dough into 12 equal pieces. Roll or press out each piece into a round, about ½ inch thick and 5 inches across. Place 1 tablespoon of filling on each round. Draw up into the shape of a triangle (see illustration). Be careful not to get juice on the edges of the dough. Dip your fingers in flour as needed to prevent them from getting sticky.

Brush cookie sheets or rectangular cake pans with olive oil, and place the pies in rows. Bake until golden brown, about 20 minutes. You can also broil them for 5 minutes to bring out more color.

Makes 3 dozen pies

Each: calories: 171, protein: 4 gm., carbohydrates: 16 gm., fat: 2 gm.

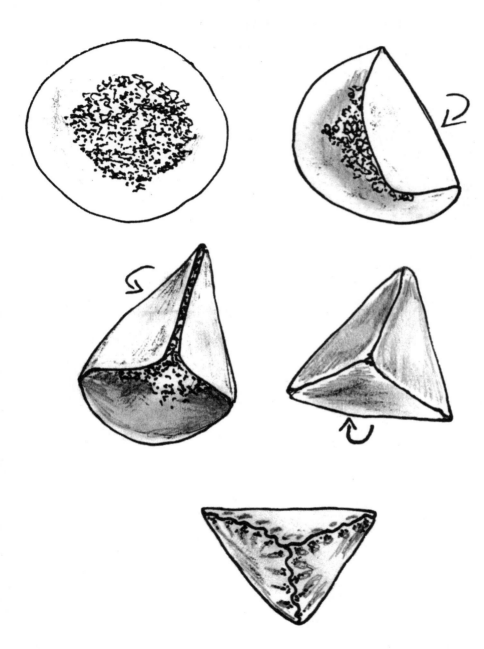

Spinach with Onion in Olive Oil
Sbanegh Bi-Zeyt
سبانغ بزيت

2 cups water
2 bunches spinach, well washed and
  coarsely chopped

2 medium onions, julienned
½ cup olive oil or canola oil
6 cloves garlic, minced

2 teaspoons salt
½ cup fresh lemon juice

Bring the water to a boil in a medium saucepan. Blanch the spinach by cooking it for 2 minutes in the water, then remove and strain. Squeeze out any excess water by pressing the spinach in a colander.

Sauté the onions in the olive oil until lightly brown. Remove some of the onions, and save for a garnish. Add the garlic and stir well until golden brown.

Add the spinach and salt, and stir gently but thoroughly. Sprinkle with the lemon juice.

Arrange the spinach in a large, shallow plate, and garnish with the reserved onions. You can serve this hot or cold.

Serves 4-6

Per serving: calories: 271, protein: 4 gm., carbohydrates: 11 gm., fat: 27 gm.

Yogurt in Mint Sauce
Labneyeh
لبنية

This is our mom's favorite recipe. She likes this especially in the summer.

2 tablespoons cornstarch, combined with in ¼ cup water
½ gallon plain non-fat yogurt

1 cup uncooked white rice
2 teaspoons salt

8 cloves garlic, minced
1 tablespoon crushed dried mint leaves

Mix the cornstarch and water with the yogurt, and stir well. Cook over low heat in a heavy-bottomed pot, stirring continuously, until the mixture thickens and reaches a creamy consistency. Be careful; don't burn the yogurt!

Add the rice and salt, and cook over very low heat until the rice is tender, about 1 hour.

Mix the garlic with the mint, and add to the rice once it is done. Cook for 5 more minutes, then immediately serve in bowls, or refrigerate the bowls and serve cold.

Serves 6
Per serving: calories: 249, protein: 22 gm., carbohydrates: 39 gm., fat: 0 gm.

Zucchini Omelet
Ojhet Al-Koosa
عجة الكوسى

6 large eggs
½ cup finely chopped fresh parsley

½ cup finely chopped onions
1 teaspoon salt
½ teaspoon allspice

2½ cups peeled zucchini
1 cup boiling water

3 tablespoons flour
½ teaspoon cinnamon
2 tablespoons oil

Beat the eggs lightly with a fork, then add the parsley. Rub the onions with ½ teaspoon salt and ½ teaspoon allspice. Drain off any juice from the onions. Add to the egg mixture, and stir.

Add the zucchini to the 1 cup of boiling water. Simmer for 5 minutes, then drain. Add the remaining ½ teaspoon salt and the zucchini to the eggs. Blend in the flour and cinnamon, and mix gently.

Heat some olive oil in a frying pan to sizzling. Drop in ¼ cup of the batter, and fry until golden brown. Turn over and fry the other side. Remove from the oil and drain on paper towels.

Serve the omelets inside pita bread. Add any vegetables you like. We use tomatoes, pickles, diced radishes, green pepper, and sliced onions.

Serves 4-6

Per serving: calories: 170, protein: 9 gm., carbohydrates: 6 gm., fat: 12 gm.

Zucchini Stew
Mnazalet Al-Koosa
منذلة الكوسى

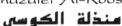

One of Dalal's favorites! This recipe is delicious and very easy to make.

2 large zucchini, peeled and finely chopped
¼ cup olive oil

1 medium white onion, chopped

2 large ripe tomatoes, peeled and diced
½ teaspoon allspice
½ teaspoon cinnamon
1½ teaspoons salt

3 medium eggs

Sauté the zucchini in the olive oil until golden. Remove the zucchini and set aside. Place the onion in the same pan, and sauté until light golden. Add the sautéed zucchini, tomatoes, and seasonings. Cover the pan and simmer for 15 minutes.

Add the eggs and cook for 5 more minutes, stirring as the eggs congeal.

Serve warm or cold with a plate of your favorite vegetables and olives.

Serves 4
Per serving: calories: 224, protein: 7 gm., carbohydrates: 9 gm., fat: 17 gm.

From the Tables of Lebanon

Sandwiches

Aroos

سندويش

Cauliflower Sandwiches
Aroosat Arnabeet Meklee
عروسة أرنبيط مقلي

3 cups water
1 medium cauliflower, split into small
  flowerettes
1 teaspoon salt

¾ cup canola oil

2 loaves Arabic bread
1 cup of your favorite vegetables

Bring the water to a boil, add the cauliflower and salt, and cook for 5 minutes. Remove and drain well.

Heat the canola oil in a large sauté pan, and fry the cauliflower until golden brown. Remove and arrange on paper towels to drain the excess oil.

Split open the Arabic breads, and top one side with cauliflower. Add any other vegetables and toppings you like, and roll like a burrito.

Serve hot.

Serves 2

Per serving: calories: 424, protein: 8 gm., carbohydrates: 35 gm., fat: 27 gm.

Eggplant Sandwiches
Aroosat Batinjan Meklee
عروسة باتنجان مقلي

1 large eggplant, peeled and sliced
  1 inch thick
2 quarts water
1 teaspoon salt

½ cup canola oil

2 pita breads
1 medium tomato, cut in wedges
1 cup chopped fresh mint leaves,
½ small white onion, julienned

Soak the eggplant in the water and salt for 40 minutes, and drain.

Heat the canola oil and fry the eggplant until golden brown, flipping several times. Arrange on paper towels to drain the excess oil.

Split open the pita breads, and top with the eggplant, tomato wedges, mint leaves, and onion. Roll like a burrito and eat.

Serves 2

Per serving: calories: 361, protein: 8 gm., carbohydrates: 48 gm., fat: 14 gm.

Falafel Sandwiches
Falafel
فلافل

4 pita breads

12 Falafel, pg. 101
8 slices ripe tomatoes
2 slices cucumber pickles
4 radishes, sliced
½ cup chopped fresh parsley
½ cup Tahini Sauce, pg. 32

Warm the pita breads in a 200°F oven for about 5 minutes. Cut each bread in half. Stuff the falafel, vegetables, and parsley inside the breads evenly, as if you're filling a taco. Drizzle the Tahini Sauce on top.

Variation: Instead of cutting the bread in half, split the bread by inserting a knife in the middle. Lay a falafel on one side of a piece of bread and the vegetables on the other side. Drizzle the Tahini Sauce on top, and roll like a burrito.

Serves 4

Per serving: calories: 812, protein: 21 gm., carbohydrates: 98 gm., fat: 36 gm.

Fried Potato Sandwiches
Aroosat Batata Mekleeyee

عروسة باطاطا مقلية

1 cup canola oil
**4 medium potatoes, peeled and
  julienned ½ inch thick**

4 pita breads
3 medium tomatoes, sliced
½ cup fresh mint leaves

Heat the canola oil in a frying pan, and fry the potatoes until golden brown. Remove and arrange on paper towels to drain the excess oil.

Split open the pita breads, and stuff with the potatoes, tomatoes, and mint. You can substitute any of your favorite vegetables for the tomatoes and mint.

Serve hot.

Serves 4
Per serving: calories: 403, protein: 8 gm., carbohydrates: 59 gm., fat: 14 gm.

Thyme Pies
Manakich Bi-Zaatar
مناقيش بزعتر

Zaatar is a seasoning blended from thyme, salt, sumac, and toasted sesame seeds. It is available at most Lebanese and Middle Eastern grocery stores.

½ cup zaatar
3 tablespoons extra-virgin olive oil
1 recipe Arabic Bread dough (page 28),
or 1 loaf frozen bread dough, thawed

Preheat the oven to 450°F. Mix the zaatar with the olive oil in a medium bowl. Add more oil if desired.

Roll the dough balls into 6-inch circles. Flute the edges to secure the filling (see illustration). Spread the zaatar mixture equally over the dough. Press the surface of the dough with your fingertips in several places.

Place the circles of dough on cookie sheets lightly oiled with olive oil. Bake for 6 minutes or until golden brown. For a more authentic crust, bake these directly on the floor of your oven.

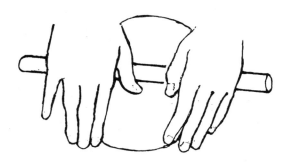

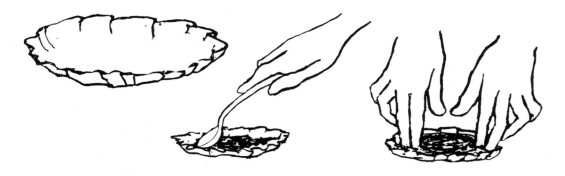

Makes 4 pies

146
Per pie: calories: 451, protein: 11 gm., carbohydrates: 69 gm., fat: 14 gm.

Drinks

Sharabat

شرابات

Lemonade
Limonada
ليمونضة

Try this delicious lemonade made from basic ingredients without any preservatives or colorings. Our loving mother, Rafica, has perfected this recipe over the last 40 years. Although she mostly serves it in the summertime, she prepares it when a family member is inflicted with the flu in the winter, or at any time by request of all her little granddaughters and grandsons: Maher, Wissam, Sandra, Carla, Aref, Yara, and Tamara!

4 large fresh lemons
1 cup white sugar
6 cups water

2 fresh oranges, squeezed (optional)
1 tablespoon orange blossom water (mazaher)

Wash the lemons very well. Cut each into 4 wedges, and place in a bowl. Sprinkle the sugar evenly over the wedges, and rub well with your fingers. Squeeze the lemons and stir the juice, lemon wedges, and sugar together. Place this mixture in a pitcher with the water, and soak for 2-3 hours.

Stir the mixture well, then strain through a strainer so that no seeds or pulp pass through into the juice. Discard the lemon rinds and pulp. Add orange juice, if desired. Add mazaher and stir well. You can adjust the sweetness to meet your taste by adding more sugar.

Chill for 3-4 hours before serving with two ice cubes per glass.

Serves 6-8

Per serving: calories: 125, protein: 0 gm., carbohydrates: 31 gm., fat: 0 gm.

Mulberry Syrup Drink
Sharab al-Toot
شراب التوت

This delicious drink is commonly served in the summer to guests and family. The syrup is available in bottles at most Lebanese and Middle Eastern stores.

1 cup mulberry syrup
4 cups water
8 ice cubes

Pour the mulberry syrup in a large pitcher. Add the water and stir thoroughly with a large spoon. Add the ice cubes.

Refrigerate for 1 hour. Stir again before serving.

Serves 4

Per serving: calories: 400, protein: 0 gm., carbohydrates: 100 gm., fat: 0 gm.

Red Rose Syrup Drink
Sharab al-Warad
شراب الورد

In addition to being served on hot summer days, this refreshing drink is served at engagement and wedding ceremonies. The syrup is available in bottles at most Lebanese and Middle Eastern stores.

1 cup red rose syrup
4 cups water
8 ice cubes

Pour the red rose syrup in a large pitcher. Add the water and stir thoroughly with a large spoon. Add the ice cubes.

Refrigerate for 1 hour. Stir again before serving.

Serves 4

Per serving: calories: 400, protein: 0 gm., carbohydrates: 100 gm., fat: 0 gm.

Banana Honey Shake
Moze Bi-Assal
موز بعسل

Dalal's son, Zane, and our brother, Chaouki, love this drink.

3 ripe bananas
2 tablespoons pure honey
4 cups milk
6 ice cubes (optional)

Place all the ingredients in a blender, and combine at a high speed until a thin, creamy consistency is reached. Serve immediately.

Serves 4

Per serving: calories: 261, protein: 9 gm., carbohydrates: 37 gm., fat: 7 gm.

Strawberry Milkshake
Fraze Bi-Halib
فريز بحليب

2 cups fresh ripe strawberries

1⅓ cups cold 1% or 2% milk
¼ cup sugar

Wash the strawberries and drain.

Combine the milk and sugar well in a blender. Add the strawberries and blend well.

Serve immediately.

Serves 3

Per serving: calories: 135, protein: 4 gm., carbohydrates: 26 gm., fat: 1 gm.

Mint Tea
Shy Al-Nanaa
شاي النعنع

4 cups water
¼ cup fresh green mint leaves
4 teaspoons tea leaves
sugar or honey to taste

Bring the water to a boil in a teakettle. Add the mint and boil for 2 minutes. Add the tea leaves and remove from the heat. Let sit for 3 minutes. Strain and serve with sugar or honey.

Makes 4 cups

Per cup: calories: 22, protein: 0 gm., carbohydrates: 5 gm., fat: 0 gm.

Coffee
Kahwe
قهوة

Although tea is served every day, the Lebanese people are coffee addicts! Invariably, coffee is served with breakfast, at social visits, with every business transaction, at weddings, at funerals . . . in practically any social setting. It is the symbol of Lebanese hospitality. For instance, if you were going by a friend's house to drop off something, you will have to come in for a quick cup!

The coffee currently served in Lebanon is commonly referred to as Turkish coffee, and in many ways it is similar to the one served in Turkey. The Lebanese buy their coffee freshly ground from toasted beans on a weekly basis. Shops that sell coffee are in great abundance, and the smell of freshly ground coffee fills many streets. Some people like their coffee with cardamom (hab al-heyl). Coffee is always made in a special piece of equipment called a raqwi (see illustration). It can be served black and bitter (such as at sad occasions and funerals), sweet (such as at weddings), or in between (mazbuta).

In the United States, you can find good quality vacuum-packed Lebanese coffee at most Lebanese or Middle Eastern grocery stores. You can also purchase a fairly inexpensive raqwi and small coffee mugs (fanajeen).

1 cup cold water
2 teaspoons cardamom seeds

3 teaspoons Lebanese coffee

2 teaspoons sugar
1 teaspoon rose water

Place the water in the raqwi. Slightly crack the cardamom seeds to release their flavor. Add to the water and bring to a boil.

Remove from the stove and add the coffee. Bring back to a boil, stirring constantly. Lift off the stove for a few seconds so that the coffee doesn't boil over. Return the raqwi to the stove, and repeat the boiling up process about three times. Stir the coffee at all times. After the final boiling, stir in the sugar and rose water.

Let the coffee settle for a few minutes before serving. Cover the top of the raqwi with a small plate to keep it hot. Pour into small demitasse cups, and enjoy with friends and family!

Note: You can adjust the amount of sugar to suit your taste.

Makes 4 demitasse size cups

Per demitasse: calories: 13, protein: 0 gm., carbohydrates: 3 gm., fat: 0 gm.

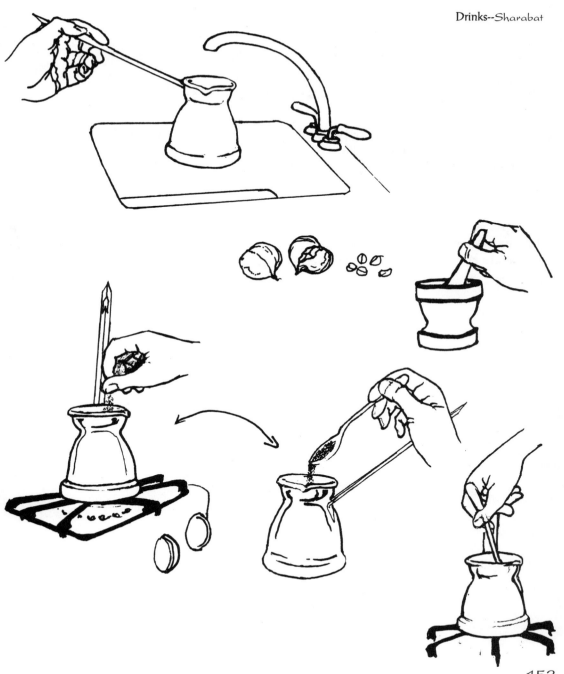

White Coffee
Kahwe Bayda
قهوة بيضاء

This simple caffeine-free drink is served in the mountains of Lebanon, especially after a meal heavy in garlic. It is very similar to mint tea. The mint in the recipe supposedly gets rid of garlic breath. Does it work! Try it and find out for yourself!

2 cups water

¼ cup fresh mint leaves
1½ teaspoons orange blossom water (mazaher)

Bring the water to a boil in a raqwi (see page 153). Remove from the heat. Add the mint leaves and orange blossom water. Let set for at least 5 minutes. Strain out the mint leaves, and serve in small demitasse cups.

Makes 2 cups

Per cup: calories: 0, protein: 0 gm., carbohydrates: 0 gm., fat: 0 gm.

Desserts

Helwayat

حلوايات

Lebanon is famous for its large selection of desserts and sweets, many of which are served during the holidays and for social occasions. Pastry and sweet shops are in great abundance in large cities. They carry a diverse range of items, from specialty chocolates to baklava. Lebanon draws on the pastry traditions of both the West and East, having acquired these traditions during the reigns of invading civilizations. But the Lebanese didn't stop at just improvising on the recipes given to them; they used their creativity and good taste to improve them. For instance, the Turks, during the Ottoman empire, introduced baklava to Lebanon. Today, Lebanon has the largest variety of baklava in the world. A visitor to any Arabic pastry shop in Lebanon will witness dozens and dozens of large, shallow plates with rows and rows of many different kinds of baklava, filled with a variety of stuffings—from pine nuts, walnuts, coconuts, and pistachios to cream.

Turkish pastry is not the only delicacy that one can savor in the cities. French pastry shops, called patisseries, exist in every big neighborhood. Mr. Jacques Meric, a friend of Maher's and former French consul to many countries including Lebanon, once told Maher that the best Foret Noire Gateau he had ever eaten was not in his native Paris, but in Beirut!

Although the majority of pastries and sweets are produced in specialty shops, many Lebanese families make their own for special occasions. For instance, during religious holidays Christians make a semolina and flour-based pastry perfumed with orange blossoms, called maamoul. The Lebanese also celebrate a new birth in the family by making a caraway-rice based pudding, called meghli. It is served in small ice cream bowls, garnished with walnuts, almonds, pine nuts, pistachios, and soaked raisins.

Recently, the Lebanese have added yet another dessert to their large selection: Italian "gelato" (ice cream)! Several shops in the cities of Beirut, Zahle, and Tripoli are producing a variety of gelato equal in quality to the best in Italy!

Baklava

Baklava

بقلاوة

Contrary to what most Americans believe, baklava is not originally Greek! Baklava originated in Turkey and was later exported to Greece, Syria, Jordan, and Lebanon. Over the last 100 years, the Lebanese people have demonstrated their amazing culinary creativity by perfecting and expanding the variety of baklava. Indeed, several dozen varieties are available in almost any Arabic pastry shop. However, the quality of baklava can vary tremendously from store to store, as it takes great skill to produce properly. In Lebanon, there are about a half dozen families which have been baking baklava for the last century or so, and their secret recipes are only transmitted from one generation to another! They sell it fresh daily in one of their many shops.

In the United States, quality baklava can be obtained by mail from Lebanese bakeries in Dearborn, Michigan (see the section on Lebanese and Middle Eastern grocery shops on pages 168-169). Or you can try to make your own using our simple recipe!

3 cups finely chopped walnuts
½ cup sugar

2 pounds filo dough
2 cups melted unsalted butter

4 cups Sweet Syrup (kater), pg. 159
1 cup ground pistachio nuts for garnish

Combine the walnuts and sugar well. Butter a 10 x 14-inch baking pan.

Divide the filo dough into two sections. Use one section for the bottom layers and the other for the top layers. Take 2 filo sheets and lay in the bottom of the baking pan. Brush melted butter on top. Add two more sheets and brush with butter again. Spoon some of the walnuts and sugar evenly over the bottom layers of filo dough, and drizzle some of the butter over the walnuts. Repeat until ½ of the filo dough is used, using up all the walnuts and sugar in the process. Layer the remaining filo sheets on top, 2 at a time, spreading butter on top of the second sheet before 2 more are added. Brush the top sheet with butter.

Using a cookie or pizza cutter, cut into 1½-inch diamond-shaped pieces. Bake at 300°F until golden brown. Remove the baklawa from the oven. Pour the cold kater evenly over the top until all the pieces are well saturated. Garnish with the ground pistachios.

Can serve hot or cold.

Makes approximately 40 small pieces

Per piece: calories: 348, protein: 3 gm., carbohydrates: 46 gm., fat: 16 gm.

Cream Cheese
Ashta
قشطة

Recipe I

1 pound ricotta cheese
¾ cup white sugar

Combine the cheese and sugar, and use as a pancake filling (see pages 161 and 162).

Recipe II

4 cups milk
1 cup cream

Place the milk and cream in a pot, and bring to a gentle boil over medium heat, stirring often. Reduce the heat to very low, and simmer for 2 hours.

Remove and let sit for about 6 hours or until the cream is thick. Refrigerate overnight and then use as a pancake filling (see pages 161 and 162).

Makes approximately 4 cups
Recipe I: Per cup: calories: 292, protein: 14 gm., carbohydrates: 40 gm., fat: 8 gm.
Recipe II: Per cup: calories: 326, protein: 10 gm., carbohydrates: 13 gm., fat: 26 gm.

Flour Balls in Syrup
Aawamat
عوامات

1 tablespoon yeast
3 cups water

4 cups regular white flour
dash of salt

4 cups canola oil

3 cups Sweet Syrup (kater), pg. 159

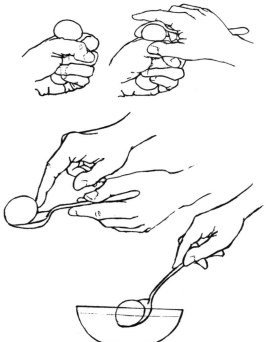

Dissolve the yeast in 1 tablespoon of luke-warm water. Set aside for 12 minutes.

Meanwhile, mix the flour and salt. Add the 3 cups water and the yeast. Mix well until the dough is smooth and elastic. Set aside in a large bowl, and cover with a piece of cloth for 4-5 hours.

Pour the canola oil into a deep frying pan, and heat over medium-low heat. Take the dough in your left hand, and gently squeeze the dough up between your thumb and forefinger, forming small, wal-nut-sized balls (see illustration). Using a teaspoon, scoop the ball out of your hand, and drop into the heated oil. Turn several times to insure that all the sides are equal-ly browned. Once they are golden brown, remove and drain the excess oil.

Dip the fried flour balls into kater, and leave for a few minutes so that each one absorbs some kater. Remove and place in a shallow plate.

May be served warm or cold.

Serves 10

158

Per serving: calories: 691, protein: 5 gm., carbohydrates: 143 gm., fat: 10 gm.

Sweet Syrup
Kater
قطر

3 cups sugar
1 cup water

½ tablespoon fresh lemon juice
½ cup orange blossom water

Combine the sugar and water in a small saucepan, and heat over medium until boiling, about 10-15 minutes. Once thickened, add the lemon juice and orange blossom water. Stir and remove from the stove right away. Let cool to room temperature.

It is best to pour cold kater over a warm dessert than the other way around.

Makes 1½ cups

Per ¼ cups: calories: 360, protein: 0 gm., carbohydrates: 90 gm., fat: 0 gm.

Mastika Corn Flour and Milk Pudding
Kachtaleyeh
قشطلية

Mastika or "mistki" is a powder made from evergreen resin. The plain resin is often used as a chewing gum to freshen the breath. As a powder, it is added to ice creams and desserts to give a distinctive flavor.

1 gallon whole milk
2¼ cups corn flour

¼ teaspoon mastika (mistki)
½ teaspoon rose water
½ teaspoon orange blossom water

1 cup Sweet Syrup (kater), pg. 159
2 cups ground pistachios

Place the milk in a large, heavy pot, and add the corn flour. Stir well before heating. Cook over medium-low heat, stirring continuously. Bring to a gentle boil. Lower the heat and simmer for 10 minutes.

Pound the mastika with a mortar until it becomes a powder. Add to the milk and stir. Add the rose water and orange blossom water, and stir. Let set 5 more minutes in the pot.

Pour the pudding into pudding dishes, and let cool at room temperature. Chill in the refrigerator for 4-6 hours.

When chilled, remove from the refrigerator, spoon the honey syrup on top, and garnish with the ground pistachios.

Variations: Whole, peeled pistachios can be used. Soak first in cold water for about 2 hours, drain, and use to garnish the pudding.

Serves 10-12

Per serving: calories: 531, protein: 19 gm., carbohydrates: 57 gm., fat: 24 gm.

Pancakes with Creamy Cheese Filling
Katayeef Bi-Ashta
قطايف بقشطة

¼ cup warm water
1 teaspoon sugar
2 teaspoons dried yeast

2 cups flour
¼ teaspoon salt
1½ cups lukewarm water

¼ cup canola oil
One recipe Cream Cheese (ashta),
  pg. 157
1½ cups Sweet Syrup (kater), pg. 159

Place the ¼ cup warm water in a bowl, and add the sugar. Stir well. Add the yeast and stir until dissolved. Set aside to rise for 5 minutes.

Sift the flour and salt into a large bowl. Make a hole in the center of the flour, pour in the 1½ cups water and the yeast mixture, and mix well with the flour to form a smooth batter. Cover with a piece of cloth, and let rise for 1 hour.

Grease a skillet with a paper towel soaked in canola oil. Heat the skillet until a drop of water flicked onto it dances across the surface. Pour about 2½ tablespoons of batter on for each pancake. Spread the batter about 3½ inches in diameter. Cook only one side of the pancake until lightly browned and bubbles have formed on the top. Remove and place on a large shallow plate. Repeat with more batter until all of it is used up.

Spread 1½ tablespoons of the cream cheese filling on the uncooked side of each pancake, and fold in half. Firmly pinch the edges together to seal, and fold in the ends to form a crescent (see illustration). Drizzle hot syrup over and serve hot.

Serves 6
Per serving: calories: 821, protein: 14 gm., carbohydrates: 148 gm., fat: 18 gm.

Pancakes with Walnut Filling
Katayeef Bi-Joz
قطايف بجوز

¼ cup warm water
1 teaspoon sugar
2 teaspoons dried yeast

2 cups flour
¼ teaspoon salt
1½ cups water

¼ cup canola oil

Filling:
2 cups ground walnuts
½ cup sugar
1 teaspoon ground cinnamon
2 teaspoons orange blossom water
1 recipe Cream Cheese (ashta), pg. 157

1½ cups Sweet Syrup (kater), pg. 159

Place the warm water in a bowl and add the sugar; stir well. Add the yeast and stir until dissolved. Set aside to rise for 5 minutes.

Sift the flour and salt into a large bowl. Make a hole in the center of the flour, pour the water and yeast mixture into the center, and mix well with the flour to form a smooth batter. Cover with a piece of cloth, and let rise for one hour.

Grease a skillet with a paper towel soaked in canola oil. Heat the skillet until a drop of water flicked onto it dances across the surface. Pour about 2½ tablespoons of batter on for each pancake. Spread the batter about 3½ inches in diameter. Cook only one side of the pancake until lightly browned and bubbles have formed on the top. Remove and place on a large shallow plate. Repeat with more batter until all of it is used up.

Mix the filling ingredients well. Spread 1½ tablespoons of filling on the uncooked side of each pancake, and fold in half. Firmly pinch the edges together to seal, and fold in the ends to form a crescent (see illustration). Drizzle hot syrup over and serve hot.

An alternative way of serving katayeef bi-joz, is by placing them on a greased baking sheet, brushing them with melted butter, and baking them at 350°F for 10 minutes or until golden brown. Another option is to deep fry them in 4 cups of canola oil before adding the kater. Once fried to a deep brown color, they can be removed and the excess oil drained on paper towels. Kater is then poured over the fried katayeef. Both of these alternative ways are delicious, but if you're watching your weight, you'd better stick to the simple version above.

Yield: 3 dozen pancakes

Per pancake: calories: 182, protein: 3 gm., carbohydrates: 28 gm., fat: 6 gm.

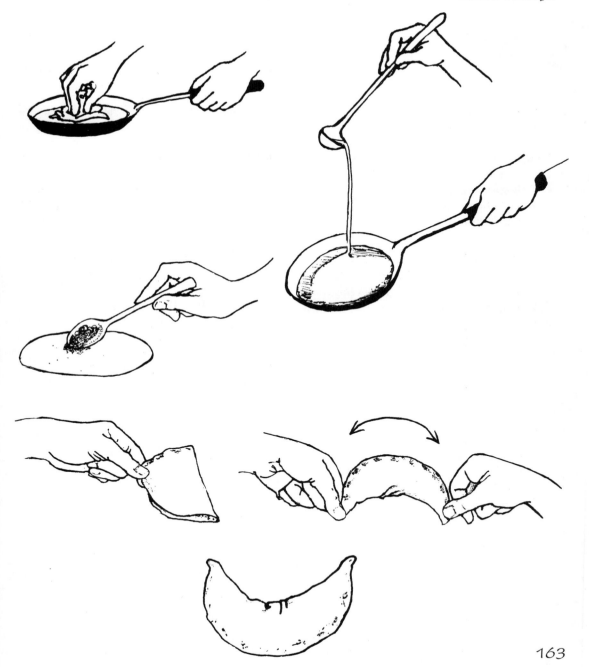

163

Powdered Rice Pudding
Meghli
مغلي

Meghli is an authentic Lebanese dessert served at many occasions, but especially when there is a new birth in a family.

1 cup powdered rice (baby's rice)
1½ cups sugar
1 tablespoon ground cinnamon
½ teaspoon caraway seeds
6 cups cold water

1 cup shredded coconut
2 cups non-salted, non-roasted nut mixture, soaked overnight—walnuts, pine nuts, almonds, raisins, pistachios

Combine the powdered rice, sugar, cinnamon, and caraway seeds in a large, heavy pot. Add the water and stir well. Cook over medium heat, stirring constantly until the mixture starts to thicken, usually about 30 minutes. Stir constantly so the bottom does not burn. Simmer for an additional 10 minutes over low heat.

Pour into pudding dishes, cool to room temperature, then chill in the refrigerator for about 4-6 hours.

When ready to serve, garnish with the shredded coconut first and then the drained nut mixture. Meghli can be kept in the refrigerator for several days.

Serves 6

Per serving: calories: 749, protein: 9 gm., carbohydrates: 97 gm., fat: 36 gm.

Rice Pudding
Riz Bi-Halib
رز بحليب

2 cups uncooked white rice
3 cups water

1 gallon whole milk
1 cup cornstarch
1 tablespoon powdered rice

2-3 cups sugar
2 tablespoons rose water

Wash the rice and soak in cold water for 30 minutes. Drain and place in a large, heavy pot. Add the water and cook over medium heat until the rice is soft but not mushy.

In a separate bowl, mix the milk, cornstarch, and powdered rice. Add to the pot and cook over medium heat for about 25 minutes, stirring constantly so the bottom does not burn.

Add the amount of sugar suggested above or adjust to the desired sweetness. Add the rose water and cook for 5 more minutes.

Pour into small pudding bowls. Cool to room temperature, then chill in the refrigerator for about 4-6 hours. Serve chilled when ready. Riz bi-halib will last several days in the refrigerator.

Variation: Orange blossom water may be substituted for the rose water, if desired.

Makes 10-12 servings
Per serving: calories: 536, protein: 15 gm., carbohydrates: 92 gm., fat: 11 gm.

Semolina Dessert
Nammura
نمّورة

1 tablespoon tahini

4 cups semolina or cream of wheat
1 cup plain yogurt
2 cups sugar
3 teaspoons baking powder

½ cup shredded coconut
½ cup blanched almonds

1 cup Sweet Syrup (kater), pg. 159

Preheat the oven to 350°F. Grease a 13 x 9-inch cake pan with the tahini.

Mix the semolina, yogurt, sugar, and baking powder. Pour the mixture into the pan, and spread evenly. Sprinkle the coconut and almonds on top.

Bake until golden brown, about 45 minutes. Don't overbake, as the nammura will get too hard.

When done, cut into small squares while still in the pan. Spoon cold honey syrup over the hot nammura. Let cool to room temperature for 1 hour, then serve.

Makes about 36 small squares

Per square: calories: 137, protein: 1 gm., carbohydrates: 25 gm., fat: 3 gm.

Glossary of Spices, Herbs, and Other Ingredients

Spices and herbs can contribute tremendously to the success or failure of a dish. The Lebanese have mastered the art of combining spices and herbs in a variety of dishes to produce exceptional aromas and flavors. The abundance and variety of spices and herbs grown in Lebanon or imported from the East have made this possible. Practice, time, and a little bit of luck are key in the success and production of delicious meals! We hope that you will prepare many of our recipes and discover the delicious possibilities of spices and herbs.

But don't be limited to our recipes, as they are not etched in stone. After you try our original version once, add or delete spices and herbs according to your personal taste. The Lebanese do that all the time. When doing so, keep in mind the following: some spices add a distinctive flavor to food (i.e. bay leaves, parsley, mint, saffron, thyme, sumac, rose and orange blossom waters), some sharpen the taste (i.e. garlic, mustard, onions, lemon juice, tomato sauce), and some improve the taste (i.e. red, black, & white peppers, allspice, nutmeg, cinnamon, cumin, cloves).

Anise seed *(anis)* - Anise is native to the western Mediterranean and is one of the oldest known seasonings. The slightly licorice-flavored seeds of a small plant are used in cakes, breads, and a popular Lebanese drink called arak. The seeds release even more flavor when ground or crushed.

Bay leaves *(laurier)* - These smooth, shiny evergreen leaves (also known as bay laurel) are found all over the Mediterranean and are native to the region. They are delicious with a variety of foods, especially vegetables. The dried leaves can be used whole or in flakes and are a strong flavoring; one leaf will flavor a gallon of broth. Fresh leaves make a nice garnish.

Black cherry kernels *(mahaleb)* - A sweet, Syrian spice used in breads and sweets.

Cardamom *(cardamone)* - A pungent, fragrant spice good for sweet dishes (such as halva), as well as spicy vegetable dishes, introduced to the Middle East from India. It is also used to flavor coffee. You can purchase it already ground, but in this form it loses its potency quickly.

Coriander *(cariander)* - Along with garlic, fresh coriander is a favorite herb in Lebanon and is a native plant to that region. Also known as cilantro and Chinese parsley, it has a distinct flavor that can be an acquired taste. The ground seeds have a very different flavor and are sometimes used as a table spice in the Middle East.

Cumin *(cumin)* - A strong, slightly bitter aromatic herb native to the Mediterranean, good in spicy vegetable dishes. The whole seeds are delicious when roasted in a dry frying pan.

Fennel *(fenouil)* - A native plant of Lebanon, the seeds are the most strongly flavored part and resemble anise. It is thought that they help make beans more digestible when the two are cooked together. Fennel seeds are a good addition to soups, sauces, and pastries.

Mistiki *(mastic)* - Made from the sweet gum of an evergreen, this powder is used in ice cream and desserts.

Orange blossom water *(eau de fleur d'oranger)* - Made from the blossoms of the bitter orange tree which are dried and distilled into an essence. It is added as a flavoring to desserts and other foods.

Rose water or maward *(eau de rose)* - Made from the distilled petals of Damask roses and used in desserts and sweets.

Sumac *(sumac)* - Sour lemony sumac berries are crushed for use in salads and vegetable dishes.

Tahini *(tahini)* - A paste made from toasted sesame seeds

Turmeric *(curcuma)* - A powder processed from a dried rhizome (underground stem) of the ginger family. It imparts a bright yellow color to the foods it is cooked with, similar to saffron, and has a strong, zesty flavor.

Lebanese and Middle Eastern Food Markets and Restaurants

The following is a list of grocery stores, food markets, and restaurants where you can find some or all of the ingredients described in this book. While we have taken every care to insure the accuracy of this information, we cannot guarantee it.

Some of the places mentioned below are strictly Lebanese while others are Middle Eastern stores that carry Lebanese food products. It is impossible to provide you with a comprehensive list, but we hope that it will be a starting point for you. If you locate one of these stores, they may connect you with others in your state. If you come across places not mentioned in our book, we would appreciate it very much if you would write to us at the address of the publisher on page 2, and provide us with any additional or updated information.

Arizona
Hajji Baba Middle-Eastern Market & Restaurant
1513 East Apache Blvd
Tempe, Arizona 85281
(602) 894-1905

California
Levant International Food Co.
9421 Alondra Boulevard
Bellflower, California 90706
(310) 920-0623

Falafel of Capitola
2121 41st Avenue
Capitola, California
(408) 479-9963

Sunflower Produce & Deli
20774 East Arrow Highway
Covina, California 91724
(818) 339-1141

Fresno Deli
2450 E. Gettysburg Ave
Fresno, California
(209) 225-7906

Rose International Gourmet Market
1060 Castro Street
Mountain View, California 94040
(415) 960-1900

Avo's Armenian Bakery
6740 Reseda Boulevard #C
Reseda, California 91335
(818) 774-1032

Petra Restaurant
550 Taylor Avenue
San Bruno, California
(415) 873-0966

Grapeleaf Restaurant
4031 Balboa Street
San Francisco, California
(415) 668-1515

Pasha
1516 Broadway
San Francisco, California 94123
(415) 885-4477

International Food Bazaar
2052 Curtner Avenue
San Jose, California 95124
(408) 559-3397

Middle East Food
26 Washington Street
Santa Clara, California 95050
(408) 248-5112

Falafel Hut
309 Beach Street
Santa Cruz, California
(408) 423-0567

Falafel of Santa Cruz
1501 Mission Street
Santa Cruz, California
(408) 459-0486

Shaharazad Restaurant
360 Oyster Point Blvd
South San Francisco
(415) 588-8209

Caravan Bakery
33300 Western Avenue
Union City, California 94587
(510) 487-2600

Sweis International Market
6807 Hazeltine Avenue
Van Nuys, California 91405
(818) 785-8193

Colorado
International Market
2020 South Parker Road
Denver, Colorado 80231
(303) 695-1090

Middle-East Market
2254 South Colorado Blvd
Denver, Colorado 80222
(303) 756-4580

Georgia
Basil's Mediterranean Cafe
2985 Grand Avenue NE
Atlanta, Georgia 30335
(404) 233-9755

Jaffa Gate
245 Peachtree Center Avenue NE
Atlanta, Georgia 30303
(404) 577-0352

Jaffa Gate
1197 Peachtree Street NE
Atlanta, Georgia 30303
(404) 876-0094

Lawrence's Cafe & Restaurant
2888 Buford Hwy NE
Atlanta, Georgia 30329
(404) 320-7756

Nicola's Restaurant
1602 Lavista Road NE
Atlanta, Georgia 30329
(404) 325-2524

Pars Persian Restaurant
215 Copeland Road
Atlanta, Georgia 30342
(404) 851-9566

The Cedar Tree
1565 North Decatur Road NE
Atlanta, Georgia 30307
(404) 373-2118

Middle-East Baking Company & Grocery
4000-B Pleasantdale Road
Doraville, Georgia 30340
(770) 448-9190

Salar Restaurant and Bakery
5920 Rosewell Road
Sandy Springs, Georgia 30328
(404) 252-8181

Illinois
Holy Land Bakery & Grocery
3825 N Kedzie Av
Chicago, Illinois
(773) 588-7414

Middle-Eastern Bakery & Grocery
1512 West Foster Avenue
Chicago, Illinois 60640
(773) 561-2224

Massachusetts
Near East Baking Company
5268 Washington Street
West Roxbury, Massachusetts 021132
(617) 327-0217

Michigan
Al-Salam Restaurant
10394 West Warren Ave
Dearborn, Michigan 48126
(313) 846-9190

Shatila Food Products and Pastries
6912/6914 Schaefer Road
Dearborn, Michigan 48126
(313) 582-1952

Shatila Food Products and Pastries
8505 W. Warren Ave
Dearborn, Michigan
(313) 934-1520

Minnesota
Aladdin Cafe
704 Hennepin Avenue
Minneapolis, Minnesota 55418
(612) 338-6810

Emily's Lebanese Deli
641 University Avenue NE
Minneapolis, Minnesota 55418
(612) 379-4069

Falafel King
701 West Lake Street
Minneapolis, Minnesota 55418
(612) 824-7887

Holy Land Bakery & Grocery Deli
2513 Central Avenue NE
Minneapolis, Minnesota 55418
(612) 781-2627

Java Rest
2801 Nicollet Avenue
Minneapolis, Minnesota 55418
(612) 870-7871

Joe's Market & Deli
1828 Como Avenue SE
Minneapolis, Minnesota 55418
(612) 331-1272

Mediterranean Deli
523 Cedar Avenue South
Minneapolis, Minnesota 55418
(612) 338-8646

Missouri
Campus Eastern Foods
408 Locust Street #B
Columbia, Missouri 65201
(573) 875-8724

New Jersey
Fattal's Syrian Bakery
975 Main Street
Paterson, New Jersey 07503
(201) 742-7125

Nouri's Syrian Bakery and Grocery
999 Main Street
Paterson, New Jersey 07503
(201) 279-2388

New York
Oriental Grocery
170-172 Atlantic Avenue
Brooklyn, New York 11021
(718) 875-7687

Sahadi Importing Company
187 Atlantic Avenue
Brooklyn, New York 11201
(718) 624-4550

Sahadi Importing Company
4619 2nd Ave
Brooklyn, New York
(718) 439-7779

North Carolina
Nur Deli
2810 Hillsborough St
Raleigh, North Carolina 27606
(919) 832-6255

Ohio
Gus's Middle-Eastern Bakery
308 East South Street
Akron, Ohio 44311
(330) 253-4505

Holy Land Imports
12831 Lorain Avenue
Cleveland, Ohio 44111
(216) 671-7736

Middle-East Foods
1957 West 25th Street
Cleveland, Ohio 44113
(216) 861-1803

Sinbad Food Imports
2620 North High Street
Columbus, Ohio 43202
(614) 263-2370

Byblos
1050 South Reynolds Rd
Toledo, Ohio 43615
(419) 382-1600

Oklahoma
Mediterranean Imports and Health Foods
3631 North MacArthur Blvd
Oklahoma City, Oklahoma 73122
(405) 789-5093

Pennsylvania
Bitar's
947 Federal Street
Philadelphia, Pennsylvania 19147
(215) 755-1121

Tennessee
Global Market
1513 Church St
Nashville, Tennessee
(615) 327-3682

Texas
Phoenicia Bakery and Deli
2912 South Lamar Street
Austin, Texas 78704
(512) 447-4444

Worldwide Foods
1907 Greenville Avenue
Dallas, Texas 75206
(214) 824-8860

Worldwide Foods
2419 Farrington St
Dallas, Texas
(214) 634-7700

Droubi's Bakery and Grocery
7333 Hillcroft Street
Houston, Texas 77081
(713) 988-5897

Virginia
Mediterranean Bakery
352 South Picket Street
Alexandria, Virginia 22304
(703) 751-0030

Aphrodite Greek Imports
5886 Leesburg Pike
Falls Church, Virginia 22041
(703) 931-5055

Halalco
108 East Fairfax Street
Falls Church, Virginia 22046
(703) 532-3202

Index

Arabic Index

Dalal A. Holmin

Mrs. Holmin was born and raised in Lebanon. She learned her cooking skills first hand from her mother and grandmother. She pursued her cooking degree at Mankato Vocational School in Minnesota. She has held several cooking positions at various hotels in Minnesota. She is currently pursing a degree in French studies. Dalal lives in Mankato with her husband, Leon, her three sons, Mohammad, Mazen, and Zane, and her stepson Landon.

Maher A. Abbas, M.D.

A native of Lebanon, Dr. Abbas grew up in the hills overlooking the Mediterranean sea and covered with some of the biblical olive trees. He pursued his undergraduate studies at Emory University (Atlanta, Georgia) where he obtained two degrees in biology and chemistry and graduated with several academic honors, including Phi Beta Kappa. While at Emory, he represented Lebanon in the 1988 Seoul Olympic Games as a member of the Track and Field team.

Dr. Abbas was awarded his medical degree from Stanford University Medical School in Palo Alto, California. He was the recipient of the American Federation Clinical Research Award and the Stanford University Dean's Award for Research in Cardiovascular Research Center of Stanford University. He served his internship at the Mayo Clinic and his residency at Stanford University Hospital. He is currently in the department of surgery at the Mayo Clinic (Scottsdale, Arizona). Dr. Abbas is the author of four other books, two on diet and nutrition, *Olive Oil Cookery: The Mediterranean Diet* and *College Students On the Go: Introduction to Healthy Living*, and two medical novels, *Beyond the Magic Scalpel* and *Children of Ambiguity*.

Ask your store to carry these books

Also by Maher A. Abbas, M.D. and Marilyn J. Spiegl:
Olive Oil Cookery: The Mediterranean Diet $10.95

Almost No-Fat Holiday Cookbook 12.95
A Taste of Mexico 11.95
Chef Neil's International Vegetarian Cookbook 5.00
Cooking Southern Vegetarian Style 12.95
Delicious Jamaica! 11.95
Fabulous Beans 9.95
Flavors of India 12.95
From a Traditional Greek Kitchen 12.95
From the Tables of Lebanon 12.95
From the Global Kitchen 11.95
Good Time Eatin' in Cajun Country 9.95
Indian Vegetarian Cooking At Your House 12.95
New Farm Vegetarian Cookbook 8.95
The Now and Zen Epicure 17.95
The Shiitake Way 9.95
Soyfoods Cookery 9.95
Tofu Cookery 15.95
Tofu Quick & Easy 8.95
The Tempeh Cookbook 10.95

or you may order directly from:

The Book Publishing Company
P.O. Box 99
Summertown, TN 38483

Or call: 1-800-695-2241

Please add $2.50 per book for shipping